Bloom's BioCritiques

Bloom's BioCritiques

WALT WHITMAN

Edited and with an introduction by
Harold Bloom
Sterling Professor of the Humanities
Yale University

CHELSEA HOUSE
P U B L I S H E R S
A Haights Cross Communications Company

Philadelphia

10 9 8 7 6 5 4 3 2 1

Library of Congress Cataloging-in-Publication Data

Walt Whitman / edited and with an introduction by Harold Bloom.
        p. cm. -- (Bloom's biocritiques)
Includes bibliographical references and index.
ISBN 0-7910-6377-1
  I. Whitman, Walt, 1819–1892--Criticism and interpretation. I. Bloom,
Harold. II. Series.
  PS3238 .W354 2002
  811'.3--dc21
                                        20020011621

Chelsea House Publishers
1974 Sproul Road, Suite 400
Broomall, PA 19008-0914

http://www.chelseahouse.com

Contributing editor:. Matt Longabucco

Cover design by Keith Trego

Cover: © CORBIS

Layout by EJB Publishing Services

CONTENTS

User's Guide

These volumes are designed to introduce the reader to the life and work of the world's literary masters. Each volume begins with Harold Bloom's essay "The Work in the Writer" and a volume-specific introduction also written by Professor Bloom. Following these unique introductions is an engaging biography that discusses the major life events and important literary accomplishments of the author under consideration.

Furthermore, each volume includes an original critique that not only traces the themes, symbols, and ideas apparent in the author's works, but strives to put those works into a cultural and historical perspective. In addition to the original critique is a brief selection of significant critical essays previously published on the author and his or her works followed by a concise and informative chronology of the writer's life. Finally, each volume concludes with a bibliography of the writer's works, a list of additional readings, and an index of important themes and ideas.

HAROLD BLOOM

The Work in the Writer

Literary biography found its masterpiece in James Boswell's *Life of Samuel Johnson*. Boswell, when he treated Johnson's writings, implicitly commented upon Johnson as found in his work, even as in the great critic's life. Modern instances of literary biography, such as Richard Ellmann's lives of W. B. Yeats, James Joyce, and Oscar Wilde, essentially follow in Boswell's pattern.

That the writer somehow is in the work, we need not doubt, though with William Shakespeare, writer-of-writers, we almost always need to rely upon pure surmise. The exquisite rancidities of the Problem Plays or Dark Comedies seem to express an extraordinary estrangement of Shakespeare from himself. When we read or attend *Troilus and Cressida* and *Measure for Measure*, we may be startled by particular speeches of Ulysses in the first play, or of Vincentio in the second. These speeches, of Ulysses upon hierarchy or upon time, or of Duke Vincentio upon death, are too strong either for their contexts or for the characters of their speakers. The same phenomenon occurs with Parolles, the military impostor of *All's Well That Ends Well*. Utterly disgraced, he nevertheless affirms: "Simply the thing I am/Shall make me live."

In Shakespeare, more even than in his peers, Dante and Cervantes, meaning always starts itself again through excess or overflow. The strongest of Shakespeare's creatures—Falstaff, Hamlet, Iago, Lear, Cleopatra—have an exuberance that is fiercer than their plays can contain. If Ben Jonson was at all correct in his complaint that "Shakespeare wanted art," it could have been only in a sense that he may not have intended. Where do the personalities of Falstaff or Hamlet touch a limit? What was it in Shakespeare that made the two parts of *Henry IV* and *Hamlet* into "plays unlimited"? Neither Falstaff nor Hamlet will be stopped: their wit, their beautiful, laughing speech, their intensity of being—all these are virtually infinite.

In what ways do Falstaff and Hamlet manifest the writer in the work? Evidently, we can never know, or know enough to answer with any authority. But what would happen if we reversed the question, and asked: How did the work form the writer, Shakespeare?

Of Shakespeare's inwardness, his biography tells us nothing. And yet, to an astonishing extent, Shakespeare created our inwardness. At the least, we can speculate that Shakespeare so lived his life as to conceal the depths of his nature, particularly as he rather prematurely aged. We do not have Shakespeare on Shakespeare, as any good reader of the Sonnets comes to realize: they do not constitute a key that unlocks his heart. No sequence of sonnets could be less confessional or more powerfully detached from the poet's self.

The German poet and universal genius, Goethe, affords a superb contrast to Shakespeare. Of Goethe's life, we know more than everything; I wonder sometimes if we know as much about Napoleon or Freud or any other human being who ever has lived, as we know about Goethe. Everywhere, we can find Goethe in his work, so much so that Goethe seems to crowd the writing out, just as Byron and Oscar Wilde seem to usurp their own literary accomplishments. Goethe, cunning beyond measure, nevertheless invested a rival exuberance in his greatest works that could match his personal charisma. The sublime outrageousness of the Second Part of *Faust*, or of the greater lyric and meditative poems, form a Counter-Sublime to Goethe's own daemonic intensity.

Goethe was fascinated by the daemonic in himself; we can doubt that Shakespeare had any such interests. Evidently, Shakespeare abandoned his acting career just before he composed *Measure for Measure* and *Othello*. I surmise that the egregious interventions by Vincentio and Iago displace the actor's energies into a new kind of mischief-making, a fresh opening to a subtler playwriting-within-the-play.

But what had opened Shakespeare to this new awareness? The answer is the work in the writer, *Hamlet* in Shakespeare. One can go further: it was not so much the play, *Hamlet*, as the character Hamlet, who changed Shakespeare's art forever.

Hamlet's personality is so large and varied that it rivals Goethe's own. Ironically Goethe's Faust, his Hamlet, has no personality at all, and is as colorless as Shakespeare himself seems to have chosen to be. Yet nothing could be more colorful than the Second Part of *Faust*, which is peopled by an astonishing array of monsters, grotesque devils, and classical ghosts.

A contrast between Shakespeare and Goethe demonstrates that in each—but in very different ways—we can better find the work in the person, than we can discover that banal entity, the person in the work. Goethe to many of his contemporaries, seemed to be a mortal god. Shakespeare, so far as we know, seemed an affable, rather ordinary fellow, who aged early and became somewhat withdrawn. Yet Faust, though Mephistopheles battles for his soul, is hardly worth the trouble unless you take him as an idea and not as a person. Hamlet is nearly every-idea-in-one, but he is precisely a personality and a person.

Would Hamlet be so astonishingly persuasive if his father's ghost did not haunt him? Falstaff is more alive than Prince Hal, who says that the devil haunts him in the shape of an old fat man. Three years before composing the final *Hamlet*, Shakespeare invented Falstaff, who then never ceased to haunt his creator. Falstaff and Hamlet may be said to best represent the work in the writer, because their influence upon Shakespeare was prodigious. W.H. Auden accurately observed that Falstaff possesses infinite energy: never tired, never bored, and absolutely both witty and happy until Hal's rejection destroys him. Hamlet too has infinite energy, but in him it is more curse than blessing.

Falstaff and Hamlet can be said to occupy the roles in Shakespeare's invented world that Sancho Panza and Don Quixote possess in Cervantes's. Shakespeare's plays from 1610 on (starting with *Twelfth Night*) are thus analogous to the Second Part of Cervantes's epic novel. Sancho and the Don overtly jostle Cervantes for authorship in the Second Part, even as Cervantes battles against the impostor who has pirated a continuation of his work. As a dramatist, Shakespeare manifests the work in the writer more indirectly. Falstaff's prose genius is revived in the scapegoating of Malvolio by Maria and Sir Toby Belch, while Falstaff's darker insights are developed by Feste's melancholic wit. Hamlet's intellectual resourcefulness, already deadly, becomes poisonous in Iago and in Edmund. Yet we have not crossed into the deeper abysses of the work in the writer in later Shakespeare.

No fictive character, before or since, is Falstaff's equal in self-trust. Sir John, whose delight in himself is contagious, has total confidence both in his self-awareness and in the resources of his language. Hamlet, whose self is as strong, and whose language is as copious, nevertheless distrusts both the self and language. Later Shakespeare is, as it were, much under the influence both of Falstaff and of Hamlet, but they tug him in opposite directions. Shakespeare's own copiousness of language is well-nigh incredible: a vocabulary in excess of twenty-one thousand words, almost eighteen hundred of which he coined himself. And of his word-hoard, nearly half are used only once each, as though the perfect setting for each had been found, and need not be repeated. Love for language and faith in language are Falstaffian attributes. Hamlet will darken both that love and that faith in Shakespeare, and perhaps the Sonnets can best be read as Falstaff and Hamlet counterpointing against one another.

Can we surmise how aware Shakespeare was of Falstaff and Hamlet, once they had played themselves into existence? *Henry IV, Part I* appeared in six quarto editions during Shakespeare's lifetime; *Hamlet* possibly had four. Falstaff and Hamlet were played again and again at the Globe, but Shakespeare knew also that they were being read, and he must have had contact with some of those readers. What would it have been like to discuss Falstaff or Hamlet with one of their early readers (presumably also part of their audience at the Globe), if you were the creator of such demiurges? The question would seem nonsensical to most Shakespeare scholars, but then these days they tend to be either ideologues or moldy figs. How can we recover the uncanniness of Falstaff and of Hamlet, when they now have become so familiar?

A writer's influence upon himself is an unexplored problem in criticism, but such an influence is never free from anxieties. The biocritical problem (which this series attempts to explore) can be divided into two areas, difficult to disengage fully. Accomplished works affect the author's life, and also affect her subsequent writings. It is simpler for me to surmise the effect of *Mrs. Dalloway* and *To the Lighthouse* upon Woolf's late *Between the Acts*, than it is to relate Clarissa Dalloway's suicide and Lily Briscoe's capable endurance in art to the tragic death and complex life of Virginia Woolf.

There are writers whose lives were so vivid that they seem sometimes to obscure the literary achievement: Byron, Wilde, Malraux, Hemingway. But most major Western writers do not live that exuberantly, and the greatest of all, Shakespeare, sometimes appears to have adopted the personal mask of colorlessness. And yet there are heroes of literature who struggled titanically with their own eras— Tolstoy, Milton, Victor Hugo—who nevertheless matter more for their works than their lives.

There are great figures—Emily Dickinson, Wallace Stevens, Willa Cather—who seem to have had so little of the full intensity of life when compared to the vitality of their work, that we might almost speak of the work in the work, rather than even of the work in a person. Emily Brontë might well be the extreme instance of such a visionary, surpassing William Blake in that one regard.

I conclude this general introduction to a series of literary bio-critiques by stating a tentative formula or principle for gauging the many ways in which the work influences the person and her subsequent, later work. Our influence upon ourselves is always related to the Shakespearean invention of self-overhearing, which I have written about in several other contexts. Life, as well as poetry and prose, is overheard rather than simply heard. The writer listens to herself as though she were somebody else, and the will to change begins to operate. The forces that live in us include the prior work we have done, and the dreams and waking visions that evade our dismissals.

HAROLD BLOOM

Introduction

The influence of Walt Whitman's poetry upon his life was absolute: a purer instance of the work in the writer hardly could be found. So disturbed was the household in which Whitman was raised, so dark the fates of his siblings, that Walt's self-creation appears a miracle.

At thirty, in 1849, Whitman returned to his family, abandoning his career as a journalist. He read and wrote, and worked at carpentering with his father and brothers. In the notebooks of 1854, we can see *Leaves of Grass* start to emerge, even as Walter Whitman, Sr. declined. In early July 1855, Whitman self-published the first edition of *Leaves of Grass*. On July 11, his father died. Ten days later, Ralph Waldo Emerson mailed Whitman his superb response to the poet's gift of *Leaves of Grass*.

Whitman and Emily Dickinson remain the greatest and most difficult of American poets. This is just as true now in the early twenty-first century as it was in the nineteenth. Dickinson is cognitively difficult: her mind is the strongest and most original among all poets in English since William Shakespeare and William Blake. Whitman did not have unusual conceptual powers, any more than Tennyson did. But, like Tennyson, Whitman is one of the geniuses of figurative language. His descendants among major American poets are very disparate: Wallace Stevens, W.C. Williams, Ezra Pound, T.S. Eliot, Hart Crane, John Ashbery, A.R. Ammons. Yet they share the legacy of Whitman's nuanced rhetoric, his "intricate evasions of as" [Wallace Stevens].

There is a clear relation between Whitman's biography and his elaborate command of all the resources of trope. An auto-didact,

Whitman's formal education ceased at eleven. He then was apprenticed as a printer's devil to newspapers, and progressed to printer and to editor. Whitman's pages of poetry in the 1855 *Leaves of Grass* have more the look of a nineteenth century American newspaper page than of a coventionally printed page of verse. William Blake, also self-educated, was apprenticed early to an engraver, and Blake's model always remained the engraved, illuminated page. Whitman did not read Blake until late in life, and then was intrigued both by the apparent similarities and by their more profound differences. The superbly multivalent title, *Leaves of Grass*, in the first place reflects nineteenth century printers' lingo. Leaves are pages, but also bundles of paper sheets, while grass is throwaway printers' stuff filling up pages. Whitman, though he sometimes pretends to literalism, is never more bewilderingly metaphorical than in the phrase "Leaves of Grass." Leaves are a major poetic fiction throughout Western tradition: they represent the fragility of individual lives, in an unbroken sequence from Homer, Virgil, Dante, Milton, and Shelley on to what Wallace Stevens calls "the fiction of the leaves." Grass is flesh in Isaiah and the Psalms: "Leaves of Grass" thus might mean a doubling of our most characteristic images of mortality.

For Whitman, grass is the more important fiction, beautifully elaborated in section 6 of *Song of Myself*. Beyond the large composite metaphor of "leaves of grass," Whitman's dominant trope is what he calls the "tally," a twig or cutting, like the sprig of lilac in the Lincoln elegy, or the calamus, aromatic underground stem of sweetflag, and the prime phallic emblem in the overtly homoerotic poems gathered together in the *Calamus* section of the third edition of *Leaves of Grass* in 1860.

These days, when the "discipline" of Queer Studies has taken its place on faculties next to Feminist Criticism, Multiculturalism, and all the other allied Resentments, it is of some importance to note that Whitman is rather more an autoerotic poet than a homoerotic one. He tallies by masturbating, and accumulates his poems by self-fulfillment. *Song of Myself*, sections 28-30, and "Spontaneous Me" are crucial instances.

Whitman's yearnings indubitably were homoerotic, but they were rarely (if ever) realized. The inhibition was not social but intensely personal: "To touch my person to some one else's is about as much as I can stand." Though the second-oldest of the eight siblings, Whitman early on became the father and mother to the seven others, four of whom were borderline or psychotic. That helped produce the characteristic

Whitmanian stance: generously open to others, but quick to close up when the integrity of his single self might suffer vastation.

The relation between Whitman the person and Walt Whitman, one of the roughs, archetypal American poet, is astonishingly complex and still defies criticism. It inspires the greatest originality in Whitman's poetry, an astonishing psychic cartography which he divides into three components: "my soul," "myself" and "the real me," also called "the me myself." The Whitmanian soul is his unknown nature, ethos or character, and derives from the Emersonian Oversoul. Rough Walt, an American bard at last, is the "myself" of *Song of Myself*:

Walt Whitman, a kosmos, of Manhattan the son,
turbulent, fleshy, sensual, eating, drinking and breeding,
No sentimentalist, no stander above men and women or apart from them,
No more modest than immodest.

That self or outered personality is a fiction, that is, the mythic Walt who is inspired to sum us all up: "Through me the afflatus emerging and surging, through me the current and index." But the true, personal self is quite otherwise:

Apart from the pulling and hauling stands what I am,
Stands amused, complacent, compassionating, idle, unitary,
Looks down, is erect, or bends an arm on an impalpable certain rest,
Looking with side-curved head curious what will come next,
Both in and out of the game and watching and wondering at it.

It is that real Me that mocks the poet Walt on the beach in "As I Ebb'd with the Ocean of Life." Dark demon or dusky brother, the Me Myself is at home with the great trope of origins in Whitman's poetry: the fourfold of Night, Death, the Mother, and the Sea. That enormous, fused metaphor haunts American poetry since, and is particularly central in Wallace Stevens and Hart Crane. It has been crucial also in poets elsewhere, who are Whitman's inheritors: D.H. Lawrence in England, Fernando Pessoa in Portugal, Federico García Lorca in Spain, Pablo Neruda in Chile, Jorge Luis Borges in Argentina, Octavio Paz in Mexico.

Whitman's poetry formed his life, from 1855 on. *Song of Myself* engendered *Crossing Brooklyn Ferry*, which in turn helped stimulate the great *Sea-Drift* elegies and the "Lilacs" lament for Abraham Lincoln. After the great decade 1855-1865, Whitman burned out. His last twenty-seven years, down to his death two-months short of turning seventy-three, sadly show him depleted by the sublime strength of his earlier poetry.

JUDITH CONNORS

Biography of Walt Whitman

THE QUINTESSENTIAL AMERICAN POET

In July, 1855, Walt Whitman published the first edition of *Leaves of Grass* incorporating new poetic forms and subject matter the likes of which the world had never before seen.

The poetry of the mid-1800's had become stagnant, incorporating little of the vigor and creativity Whitman knew existed in a growing, bustling country like America. According to Robert Polley, editor of *America the Beautiful in the Words of Walt Whitman*, "The poetry of Whitman's time had become dominated by conventionalized sentiment and romanticized morality and was restricted to a few metrical styles which encouraged shallow thinking and feeling." Over the years, Whitman himself had been guilty of writing some of this "copious dribble" as he called it, but eventually longed to experiment with new forms and feelings in his poetry.

He had set out to create a new "American poetry," one as large and lustful as he believed himself to be. Gone were traditional rhyme schemes and metered stanzas; the subject matter, too, would be bolder, more celebratory in nature than the works of his predecessors. American poetry, Whitman believed, should not "echo the melancholy complaints of the 'graveyard school' nor proliferate the moral precepts of didactic writers like Longfellow, Holmes, and Lowell. Exaggeration of style and subject [as seen up to now in American poetry] would be replaced by 'genuineness,' by respect for the way things really are." This new poetry would be, according to Polley, "Transcendental in tone, rhythmic without being metrical ... the beginning of a new mode of expression,"— a mode that Whitman would spend the rest of his life trying to perfect.

Walt Whitman was in his mid-30's when *Leaves of Grass* was first published and until that time, he had contributed little of consequence during his writing career as a journalist for several east coast newspapers including the *Brooklyn Daily Eagle, The Long Island Patriot, and The Manhattan Mirror.*

Joel L. Swerdlow in "America's Poet: Walt Whitman" writes that Whitman's "... journalism—coverage of fires, crimes, local politics, and slavery, which he called a 'fearful crime'—was solid but forgettable." (Swerdlow, 118)

The same held true for Whitman's other endeavors. Several short stories and *Franklin Evans*, a temperance novel he penned in 1842, were also undistinguished. In fact, little of the creative genius we appreciate today about Whitman was visible to his contemporaries. At best, he was ignored by fellow poets; at worst he was chastised, criticized and dismissed.

In *Leaves of Grass*, Whitman spoke to America and its' people, hoping to awaken in them a craving to become more literate—not only to read, but to *absorb* what they were experiencing. Whitman seldom strayed throughout his life's work from this basic purpose—to sing the praises of *all* of America, the ordinary and the extraordinary, so that *all* its citizens, wealthy and working man alike, could appreciate the power of the written word and celebrate the goodness of their nation. The "everyman" referred to in *Leaves* was intended to truly mean "every man": the "I" of *Song of Myself* is a collective one, including all Americans, united as one:

> I celebrate myself, and sing myself,
> And what I assume you shall assume,
> For every atom belonging to me as good belongs to you.

Whitman's poetry was certainly revolutionary, not only for its expressive language and free verse but also for the intensity of his emotions when discussing his prominent and pervasive themes of love (spiritual and physical alike) and democracy (collectively for the nation and individually for each person's own self-fulfillment). He believed America needed a new poetry, one that related to and embraced more people; Whitman felt that he was the poet who could supply that type of verse.

The preface to *Leaves of Grass* is clear about the kind of poetry that Whitman's book contained:

> The American poets are to enclose old and new
> for America is the race of races. Of them a bard is to be
> commensurate with a people.

While Whitman identified himself with all Americans and spoke to them through his poetry, it didn't appear as though many of his fellow citizens were listening. Copies of *Leaves of Grass* were mailed to America's great literary figures, many of whom either destroyed or disregarded the untitled book of poetry. Some took vehement offense to the themes of boastfulness, love, and nature Whitman explored in *Leaves*. L. Edmond Leipold, in *Famous American Poets*, states, "One eminent poet of the time read the poems with growing anger, affronted by the contents, then threw the pamphlet in the fireplace. It was trash, he said, fit only to be burned." (Leipold, 61)

Evidence of Whitman's non-acceptance in the literary community came several months after *Leaves* was published, in September 1855, when the Association of New York Publishers held a large and festive gathering celebrating the "growth and influence of American books over the past three decades."

"Everyone, it seemed was there. Among the 650 invited guests were Irving, Bryant, Longfellow, Whittier, Alice and Phoebe Cary, Susan and Anna Warner, and a host of others. But not Whitman. Apparently no one had thought to invite him." (Reynolds, 342-43).

Public reception as well for the small, anonymously published folio of twelve poems was, at best, lukewarm; and reviews were mixed. That is, with one major exception.

Upon completing his reading of Walt Whitman's first edition of *Leaves of Grass* (1855), Ralph Waldo Emerson, one of the most influential and respected literary men of his day, wrote Whitman praising the poems and finished his letter with the encouraging words, "I greet you at the beginning of a great career."

Emerson's effect on Whitman had actually taken hold ten years earlier, when Whitman, just beginning to experiment with poetry, read an essay of Emerson's lamenting the absence of a "genius" in American poetry: This essay, entitled "The Poet," was published in 1844, and expressed Emerson's hope that a new kind of bard would emerge, celebrating the ordinary, yet "incomparable," in America and its people:

> We have yet had no genius in America, with tyrannous eye, which knew the value of our incomparable materials, and saw, in the barbarism and materialism of the times, another carnival of the same gods whose picture he so admires in Homer ... Banks and tariffs, the newspaper and caucus ... are flat and dull to dull people, but rest on the same foundations of wonder as the town of Troy and the temple of Delphi ... Our log-rolling, our stumps and their politics, our fisheries, our Negroes and Indians ... the northern trade, the southern planting, the western clearing, Oregon and Texas, are yet unsung. Yet America is a poem in our eyes; its ample geography dazzles the imagination, and it will not wait long for metres.

Emerson celebrated *Leaves of Grass*, believing finally that America had produced a quintessential American poet, one who saw its diversity of race and attitude and embraced it.

"I rubbed my eyes a little to see if this sunbeam were no illusion," Emerson wrote, describing *Leaves* as "the most extraordinary piece of wit and wisdom that America has yet contributed."

Emerson continued:

> I am not blind to the worth of the wonderful gift of *Leaves of Grass*. I find it the most extraordinary piece of wit and wisdom that America has yet contributed. I am very happy in reading it, as great power makes us happy ... I give you joy of your free and brave thought. I have great joy in it. I find incomparable things said incomparably well, as they must be ... I greet you at the beginning of a great career, which must have had a long foreground, for such a start.

This generous tribute of high praise from Emerson, whom Whitman had read and admired for many years, was enough to propel Whitman to expand and refine his creative purpose in nine subsequent editions of *Leaves of Grass* from 1855 through his death in 1892.

"I was at a simmer," Whitman later said. "Emerson brought me to a boil."

Clearly, Emerson saw a spirit and worth in Whitman's writings that other literary men of his day did not. And Whitman, neither a shy nor modest man, perceived himself to be the long awaited American bard of Emerson's writings. The rest of the world remained to be convinced, however, so when Whitman realized his poetry was not being "absorbed by the whole of America" as he had hoped, he capitalized on Emerson's high praise, using his letter as a marketing tool for future editions of *Leaves*.

In the second edition of *Leaves of Grass*, released in 1856, Whitman reprinted Emerson's letter (apparently without his permission) on the book's cover in a hope to attract an audience for his work but also for "all the world to see what a truly great man thought of him." (Leipold, 61). Whitman, as is commonly recognized, was not above self-promotion.

Emerson's praise, however, was not echoed throughout the literary world and as the subject matter in successive editions of *Leaves of Grass* became more explicit and shocking, Emerson came to believe that he had given his approval prematurely. "According to Moncure Conway, 'Emerson said that if he had known his letter would be published he might have qualified his praise.'" (Reynolds, 343) Emerson's letter of 1855 was to be the only letter of praise Whitman received during his lifetime.

Regardless of his acceptance or popularity, Whitman continued to labor away at his poetry. By the time of his death in 1892, nine editions of *Leaves of Grass* had been published with the collection growing to over 250 poems, a cultural anthology of sorts of a growing America.

Today, however, Whitman is considered the premier American poet, one who broke with tradition both in his form and subject matter and cleared the way for modern poetry and free verse. Unfortunately, he was never embraced during his lifetime as a prophet; the acceptance and accolades he so desperately desired came many years after his death.

"Beginning from Paumanok"

In a quaint farmhouse tucked in the rolling hills of West Hills, Long Island, New York, a pivotal figure in American literature was born in the early-19th century. Now, the house where Walt Whitman lived until he was four years old sits on an interstate highway, shielded by a high privacy fence; however, the reverberations of his literary contributions to what has become modern poetry are far reaching and cannot be constrained by convention.

Whitman was extraordinary in his exploration of free verse and choice of themes in *Leaves of Grass*. He was hailed by Ralph Waldo Emerson, noted 19th century transcendentalist and essayist, as author of "*the* American poem" and is still considered to be among the most influential of American poets.

Although one can never exactly pinpoint when or where creativity starts, Walt Whitman's youth spent between Long Island and Brooklyn appears to have deeply and irreversibly influenced his literary genius. The Whitman family's roots are deeply imbedded in the history of Long Island, stretching back to the mid-17th century when their ancestors arrived in Suffolk County from England and Holland to start a new life.

"Whitmanland" covered nearly 500 acres in what is now West Hills and South Huntington, and several Whitman family members built residences on the parcel upon their arrival hundreds of years ago. Even today, the Whitman's influence is still very strong here; a walk down Old Walt Whitman Road and through the surrounding area, lush and verdant despite residential and commercial development, is punctuated with historic house signs indicating where Walt's relations lived. Modernity has even brought us a Walt Whitman Mall.

By the time, Walter Whitman, Sr. and Louisa Van Velsor married in 1816, their families had been in this country close to 200 years. Walter Whitman, Sr., a farmer and carpenter who "liked to sleep on floors of his own making," built a simple Federal style home in Whitmanland and it was here that on May 31, 1819, Walter, Jr. was born, the second of eight children.

The Walt Whitman Birthplace, as his first residence is now called, offers a glimpse into life in the Whitman household as well as 19th-century America. Walter Whitman, Sr. built the house by hand and it is a fine example of the architecture of the time. Restored by the state of

New York to its original 1819 appearance following a vigorous fundraising campaign—the birthplace was eventually purchased for $20,000 by the Walt Whitman Birthplace Association in 1951, $10,000 of which school children from across the state raised by collecting pennies, nickels and dimes.

The house is large and well-appointed by early American standards and many of the furnishings are original. A dining room cupboard displays earthenware and kitchen utensils; a child's handmade checkers set lays near by. The large wooden box containing the tools Walter, Sr. used in building the residence is tucked into a corner. In keeping with the times, there are no closets in the house due to the 19th-century "Closet Tax," thus each of the 3 bedrooms upstairs contains foot chests used for storing Sunday clothes. Not that a closet was really necessary—Whitman and his family, like most people of his time, had only two or three outfits and few belongings other than a toothbrush and a comb.

Children mostly helped with farm work and played outside; Whitman's love of the beach is evident in the basketful of seashells being sorted on the dining room table, while the desk he used during his time spent teaching is prominently displayed in one of the front rooms.

The front parlor, a more formal room with a carved mantelpiece, was used for special occasions and adjoined the borning room where Louisa Whitman recovered after the birth of each of her eight children. The Long Island cradle, large enough to hold two babies, is an authentic reproduction of the one used by the Whitman family and is conveniently located at the foot of his mother's feather bed.

The Whitman household was always busy, tending to farmwork and to children and their needs in an America that was growing and facing new challenges daily. It was a household that in many ways typified 19th-century America: hard-working and fiercely patriotic. Whitman, Sr. was a close friend of the elderly statesman, Thomas Paine, whose pamphlet *Common Sense* was believed to have hastened colonial uprisings and the struggles towards independence in the 1770's. Whitman, Sr. fiercely supported the ideals of the American Revolution and his devotion to patriotism was evident in the names he chose for three of his sons: George Washington Whitman, Thomas Jefferson Whitman, and Andrew Jackson Whitman. This devotion to country and unparalleled respect for the struggle for freedom it waged were absorbed by young Whitman who embraced these beliefs early in his life and later promoted them through his writings, identifying his own personal growth with that of his expanding nation:

> Walt early [in life] felt the pride of being an American. Many of his poems concern this theme, of a great expanding nation, young and virile and filled with the joy of life. It was actually an expression of his own feelings towards himself, for he regarded himself as an expression of the nation in which he lived. (Leipold, 58)

From all accounts, young Whitman was a good-natured, mild and gentle little boy who was especially attached to his mother, Louisa, and her parents, with whom he visited frequently as a small child at their large farm in Cold Spring Harbor, some 20 miles from the Whitman homestead. In the same farmhouse where his mother was born in 1795, Whitman would ride the horses raised and bred by his larger-than-life grandfather, Major Cornelius Van Velsor. Friendly with a booming voice, the Major was in sharp contrast to his wife, Naomi Van Velsor, who was a genial and gentle Quaker woman. Young Walt, who never went by his given name of Walter, enjoyed their company equally and savored being at their sprawling homestead, where he later recalled "every spot had been familiar to me as a child and a youth."

Much of Whitman's youth was spent wandering the hills and countryside of Long Island where he came to know many flowers and birds by their names and often played on the beaches chasing sea gulls and shouting to waves.

One of his favorite places to explore was Jayne's Hill, a short walk from the Whitman house yet seemingly miles away from everything. Known as the highest point of elevation on Long Island, 400.9 feet above sea level, it "afforded an extensive and pleasant view" of West Hills below. Whitman believed this to be "a romantic and beautiful spot."

In Whitman's time, ships sailing off Fire Island were visible on a clear day from Jayne's Hill, and before the trees on the northern end grew in, Connecticut was in full view. The young bard would spend hours wandering the trails and wooded slopes of the quiet, shaded hilltop exploring nature and seeking inspiration for his poetry. Today, a plaque at the mount's pinnacle pays tribute to Whitman and his works.

Throughout his life and literary career, Whitman remained deeply committed to his Long Island roots and it is here where his lifelong philosophies regarding nature, individualism, and democracy were formulated. He later in life attributed his friendly open manner, his respect for working people, and his ability to relate to doctors and dockworkers alike to the neighborliness of his native land.

Despite his wanderings and travels throughout his life, Whitman often returned to the theme of his beloved Paumanok, the name the original Indian inhabitants gave to the fish-shaped Long Island. For Whitman, using the Algonquin name was a kind of "poetic justice rendered to the long vanquished Native American tribe."

According to a plaque at the Whitman Birthplace, "The natural beauty of Long Island from the gentle call of the wild birds to the majestic seascape of the coastline was a lasting source of poetic inspiration and spiritual comfort for Whitman throughout his life."

In 1881, Whitman traveled back to West Hills with his friend and literary executor, Richard Maurice Bucke. He was excited about showing Bucke the place where many of his happy childhood days were spent. Whitman recorded this visit to the farmhouse of his birth in a short feature for the New York *Tribune*, entitled "A Week at West Hills." He wrote:

> Rode around all the old familiar spots, viewing and pondering and dwelling long upon them, everything coming back to me from fifty years, with childhood scenes. Went first to the old Whitman homestead on the upland at West Hills, and took a view eastward inclining south over the broad and beautiful lands of my grandfather and my father. There was the new house, the big oak ... and a little way off even the well-kept remains of the dwellings of my great-grandfather still standing with its mighty timbers and low ceilings ....went down nearly a mile further to the house where I was born in the fertile meadow land.

Just before Walt's fifth birthday, in 1824, the Whitman's moved their family from the serene and scenic life at West Hills where they had been so happy. It had become difficult for Walter, Sr. to support his ever-growing family as a farmer and sometime carpenter so the family settled in Brooklyn, close to all the hustle and bustle of New York City and its promise of work. The move marked a turning point in Whitman's life, exposing him to the people, experiences and emotions that would eventually be so eloquently discussed in *Leaves of Grass*.

The family lived in a house situated close to the eastern-most end of the Manhattan Bridge near the ferry and the docks. Because of the area's proximity to the harbor facilities, it became a city unto itself providing its residents with everything they needed: livery stables, tenement housing, small shops, a tavern and a slaughterhouse. It was a noisy, lively area, and Whitman loved it.

Mr. Whitman found work as a carpenter and young Walt would often watch his father cut and carve fresh wood, the smell of which he had become particularly fond.

The formal education he received was limited; records indicate that Whitman attended public school, apparently as an undistinguished student, until the age of 10 or 11, when he took a job as an errand boy. According to Robert Polley, Whitman's "real education" commenced upon leaving school:

> One of his first jobs was for a law firm where his employer helped him with handwriting and composition and sub-scribed for Whitman to a circulating library, the beginning of his real education. Whitman became a voracious reader and the range of his reading was great ... focusing his attention on the potentialities of the common man and his 'long journey' toward personal freedom and full self-development.

No greater gift could have been given to Whitman than the opportunity to feed his love of reading. He borrowed books constantly, reading *Arabian Nights* as well as novels by James Fenimore Cooper repeatedly. He inhaled the romantic writings of Sir Walter Scott and by the age of twelve was working in the printing office of a newspaper as a general helper, called a "printer's devil" and occasionally contributing "sentimental" pieces to the paper—his imagination fueled by Scott's writings. His love of the written word and the feelings it could evoke in people was deepened by his experiences here, leaving him "simmering, simmering" and awakening in him a desire to try his own hand at the craft of writing.

WHITMAN DEVELOPS HIS CRAFT

By the time he was 12 years old, Walt Whitman was already a published author and had landed in a profession that would serve to challenge him socially, politically, and intellectually while fueling his literary aspirations. As a young journalist, Whitman began to expand his social awareness and to formulate his own opinions about such issues as slavery, womens' rights, immigration, labor reforms, and capital punishment. The years he spent in journalism prior to writing *Leaves of Grass* helped him to ground many of the moral and intellectual convictions that later flowed from the powerful verse of America's "poet of democracy." (Walt Whitman Interpretive Center, West Hills, LI, NY) Whitman's first job was working in the printing office of a small Brooklyn-based newspaper, *The Long Island Patriot*, as a "printer's devil," where he penned "a few sentimental bits" for submission there. Around the age of 14, Whitman secured a better-paying and more prestigious position as a typesetter, and by the time his family moved back to the interior of Long Island, around 1834, Whitman was on his own and supporting himself. He was 15 years old.

A strapping boy who very early in his teens reached full physical maturity, Whitman blossomed in the big city atmosphere. He loved the hustle and bustle of the streets and found the ordinary everyday activities that took place there extraordinary. Whitman thrived on the confusion and chaos of city life and, even as a young man, reveled in the excitement, energy and diversity of New York City.

One of his favorite pastimes was to ride the ferry that crossed the East River from Brooklyn to Manhattan on a daily basis and to attend debating societies in the city. The ferry ride, which ceased operation in the 1920's, exposed Whitman to all kinds of people and it was here that he mixed with the "common people"—ferryboatmen and laborers—that would so pervade his best known writings. He would later say that no matter how many well-known and famous people he met, he was always "more at home with the workingman."

By the mid–1830's, Whitman was associated with one of the best Manhattan papers, *The Mirror*, and was contributing conventional poetry "pieces" for publication there. "His first poems, published in several New York newspapers—'But where, O Nature, where shall be the soul's abiding place?'—were sophomoric." (Swerdlow, 118) His poetry during this time, as well as his newspaper reporting, was undistinguished.

Whitman often used the journalist's pass given to him by *The Mirror* to attend the theatre and opera in New York City and continued to read voraciously in his free time. Romance novels and sentimental poetry combined with countless trips to debates and the cultural activities that New York City offered, helped develop Whitman's rich imagination. He continued in this vane, sporadically publishing poetry while pursuing his artistic interests, for a couple of years.

The year 1835, however, brought many changes to Whitman's life. By this time he had been living in a big city and working on his own for nearly two years. He had just, at the age of 16, secured a position as a compositor (or a journey printer) in Manhattan and sought inspiration for his poetry traveling the ferry line, talking to the dockworkers and passengers. Whitman long considered this period of his life spent experiencing city life and meeting a variety of people as the beginning of his writing career. However, The Great Fire of 1835 disrupted Whitman's life as he knew it and devastated the printing district and consequently, the printing industry, in New York City. An economic depression hit the city later that same year and with no work or income to speak of, Whitman, at the age of 17, was forced to return to his family on Long Island and attempt to adjust, once again to the rural family life he had not known for several years.

This proved to be an unsuccessful and frustrating experience for both Walt and his family, who assumed that his return to the farm meant his return to farming as a livelihood. Whitman, however, had no intention of living the life of a farmer and was not shy about letting that fact be known. Unwillingly to compromise on the lifestyle to which he had grown accustomed, Whitman outraged his family (his father particularly) by refusing to do farm work, often lounging the days away walking the beach reciting poetry or sleeping under a tree in the field. After a brief period at home, Whitman decided to work as a school master and traveled the whole of Long Island teaching in a dozen different towns during the next five years.

Many biographers believe that Whitman's years spent teaching were unproductive ones and that he was passing time until he could return to the city and his journalistic pursuits. Others, however, believe that his time in the classroom reinforced his already formed opinions about equality, and ignited a fierce support of educational reform, in particular, in Whitman. Either way, his classroom experiences had a profound effect on Whitman and his writings and it seemed to form his opinions about helping the disenfranchised, in this case, the children:

> In the summer of 1836, having just turned 17, Whitman began his teaching career on Long Island. Like many country teachers, young Walt worked under very difficult conditions for very low pay. During his four year teaching career, Whitman taught in nine different school districts stretching from Queens through Suffolk counties on Long Island. In Smithtown he taught 85 pupils in a one room school house. He became a fervent supporter of education reform and he later wrote newspaper articles on the subject. (Whitman Interpretive Center)

While teaching in the towns, Whitman was an enigma to many. He would often board with school families, many of whom found him to be a disagreeable house guest with irritating personal habits. The main charge against him was laziness, citing an unwillingness to help out around the host family's farm and little interest in providing guidance or comfort to younger children outside of the school room. This was in direct contrast to the enthusiasm and innovativeness Whitman brought to the classroom where he introduced his students to a broader and more worldly, some would say more spiritual of sorts, education than that to which they had become accustomed. His view of life and learning had been expanded by his stay in New York City and it was from this perspective that he approached the education of the Long Island children. Despite the fact that he would later comment his sojourn as a school-master was "one of my best experiences," Whitman really considered himself a writer, perhaps one who was temporarily out of work, but a writer—not a teacher—none the less.

During the five years he taught nomadically on Long Island, Whitman did not abandon his literary pursuits:

> [F]rustrated and confined by the exigencies of the schoolmaster's task, [Whitman] in the spring of 1838 abruptly left off teaching and reentered the world of

> newspaper publishing. He went to Huntington and founded
> a weekly paper he called the *Long Islander* ... a throwback to
> the old-time artisan publishing: Whitman was publisher,
> editor, compositor, pressman, and distributor of the paper all
> at once." (Reynolds, 60)

He diligently worked on his paper for over 10 months before he
sold it in the spring of 1839, apparently according to Reynolds, because
of "a temperamental aversion to entrepreneurship." The *Long Islander*,
still in publication today, is considered the paper of record for
Whitman's birthplace of West Hills.

By early 1840, Whitman had secured a position with the *Long
Island Democrat* writing a series called "Sun-Down Papers from the Desk
of a School-Master." In addition, he wrote dozens of articles on
educational reform, drawing on his experiences behind the
schoolmaster's desk.

> In these pieces, he allied himself completely with the
> education reformers by emphasizing the role of a nurturing
> physical and emotional environment in the training of
> children. He argues that American schools should be well
> ventilated and clean, that punishment should be gentle, and
> that the curriculum should be widely expanded to include
> music, art and gymnastics. (Reynolds, 63)

By late 1840, Whitman had retired from teaching and returned to
New York City. Throughout the following decade, Whitman expanded
his journalistic experience and reputation, working for many New York
City newspapers where he regularly wrote about the eccentricities of city
life. His daily routine of purposeless walks in which he could revel in the
sights and sounds of the city, afforded him the opportunity to take daily
swims and visit the local bathhouses regularly. During the early 1840's,
Whitman bounced around New York, publishing stories and sketches in
several newspapers and wrote a temperance novel, *Franklin Evans or the
Inebriate*. This book was Whitman's only novel and destined to be his
best commercial success, with over 20,000 copies sold.

In his various positions, he often altered his appearance to mirror an image he had in his mind of what writers, teachers or editors should look like. Once, while working as an editor at a small publication called *The Daily Aurora*, "Whitman set about looking like what he thought an editor should look like. He wore a frock coat and a high hat, frequenting all the places that an editor searching for material to publish would normally seek out." (Leipold, 59)

Eventually, he was fired from the *Aurora*, and once again a charge of public laziness was leveled against him. Between 1842 and 1845, Whitman worked for ten or more different New York City newspapers as a reporter or writer, many of which eventually fired him for poor work habits and a general malaise in his demeanor citing him to be, "so lazy that it takes two men to open his jaws when he speaks," said one colleague. (Swerdlow, 118).

By the mid-1840's, Whitman again found himself in Brooklyn writing for the *Long Island Star* as a special contributor covering Manhattan events such as musical and theatrical shows. This took him into the city on a regular basis and allowed him to plunge full-force into the cultural life the city offered. He looked and dressed the part of a fashionable New Yorker with a meticulous personal appearance, always well-dressed and well-groomed. The farm boy from West Hills had become a big city dandy.

Whitman also developed a particular passion for the opera, whose soaring melodies and uplifting arias reached him on an emotional and aesthetic level. One of the most memorable performances he witnessed was by the great Italian coloratura soprano Marietta Alboni later saying that attending the opera was "one of his life's rare and blessed bits of hours." Whitman himself believed that the "emotions, raptures, uplifts" of opera greatly contributed to his later ability to write *Leaves of Grass*. "It helped him develop his sense of musicality. 'But for the opera,' he once exclaimed, 'I never could have written *Leaves of Grass*.'" (Whitman Interpretive Center)

Works by Rossini, Bellini, Mozart, and Verdi were also favorites of Whitman's, who was known to burst into song frequently.

By 1846, Whitman had landed his most prestigious job to date as editor of the respected Democratic controlled *Brooklyn Daily Eagle*. It was during his stewardship there that Whitman wrote most of his literary reviews, including critiques of some of the world's best known literature by writers such as Carlyle, Emerson, Melville, Margaret Fuller, George Sand, Goethe and countless others.

An ardent Democratic supporter who had become increasingly involved in politics in 1840 during President Van Buren's unsuccessful campaign for a second term, Whitman felt comfortable expressing his democratic views in the *Eagle*.

> Like most Democrats, he was able to justify the Mexican war and he hero-worshipped Zachary Taylor. Linking territorial acquisition to personal and civic betterment, he was, in his nationalistic moods, capable of hailing the great American mission of 'peopling the New World with a noble race.' (Baym, et. al., 917)

Whitman and the Democrats parted ways, however, on the issue of the extension of slavery into the annexed Western territories. By the beginning of 1848, Whitman and his poet friend William Cullen Bryant (by livelihood, editor of the *Evening Post*) had joined the Free Soilers movement, a group opposed to the acquisition of more slave territory. Whitman exposed the Democratic party's support for the extension in various editorials he wrote and he was fired immediately for breaking with the party platform.

Later Whitman would attend the Free Soilers Convention as a delegate and edit *Brooklyn Freeman*, a newspaper supporting the Free Soilers' position that slavery should not be extended westward.

"Future years will never know the seething hell and the black infernal background of the Succession War," Whitman wrote. "The real war will never get into the books."

Always one to land on his feet, however, Whitman was not long unemployed. Between acts at a play one night, he met a Southern newspaperman, J.E. McClure, who hired him immediately as a reporter/editor for the *New Orleans Daily Crescent*. This assignment lasted briefly, only several months, and opinions vary as to why. Leipold states, "his writings here were no better than they had been in New York and the paper could not use a man of such low ability to produce readable material." (Leipold, 59). Yet Reynolds suggests that "The approach of summer was cause for concern, since the city was known to be dangerous for visiting Northerners who had little resistance to the yellow fever that often came with the hot season; and in May, Walt had a falling out with the owners of the paper over money matters." (Reynolds, 122)

Whatever the reason, Walt and his brother Jeff who accompanied him to New Orleans were soon on their way back to New York. The trip to New Orleans familiarized Whitman with much more of the country than he had ever seen. This trip was the first extensive traveling Whitman had done and was one of two long trips Whitman was to take in his life. Many years later, he visited the American West.

The summer of 1848, found Whitman back in New York City, writing poetry and living once again with his family who had relocated back to Brooklyn. With his father's health declining, Whitman was forced to provide financial assistance to the family and work off and on as a carpenter and "house builder" to do so. He continued to pursue his cultural interests in New York, still attending the opera and debating clubs, but was also developing a regular group of friends among the laborers with whom he toiled daily. He moved easily between the "roughs and the artists" but never intermingled the groups. While he was attracted to different aspects of both groups and was comfortable traveling in both circles of friends, he apparently felt that neither of the groups would have the same appreciation as he had of the other. Thus, Whitman spent his time, building houses by day and writing poetry and attending the opera by night.

Despite Whitman's financial contributions to his family, they still chastised him for his blatant disregard for regular mealtimes and household rules. Many of his days were spent reading at the library, strolling through the park or writing his poetry. It was also during this time that Whitman, largely a self-educated man, developed an intense interest in Egyptology and astronomy. Frequent visits to the Egyptian Museum on Broadway furthered his studies.

Whitman read extensively during this period and was greatly intrigued and influenced by the female writer, Frances Wright, a dynamic socialist and feminist, who lectured frequently in New York City on such issues as womens' rights, abolitionism, emancipation and birth control.

In *A Few Days in Athens* (1822), Wright explored the role of religion as a deterrent to human physical pleasure, writing that it [religion] should "liberate rather than restrain the human spirit." This position was wholly embraced by Whitman. In another of Wright's works, a little poem called *Pictures*, Whitman saw a verse and writing style as close to his own as he would ever find.

Developing a close platonic relationship, Whitman and Wright remained lifelong friends. Of her, he would later write: "I never felt so glowingly towards any other woman. She possessed herself of my body and soul."

Whitman gave up carpentry work by 1854 and devoted himself fully to "simply writing." Seeing himself more as a poet than a news-paperman, he spent time with other artists with whom he could discuss literary ideas. During the next two years, Whitman delved into writing *Leaves of Grass*, the most revolutionary poetic innovation in American literature.

THE FREE SPIRIT OF FREE VERSE

In many ways, the first two editions of *Leaves of Grass* mirrored the turmoil and chaos that was rampant through much of American society in the 1850's. With the increasing tensions between the North and the South, and the growing division between the classes, America was experiencing severe social and political growing pains.

Tensions between rich and poor, immigrant and native born, black and white, and North and South all intensified across the land in the mid-19th century and conditions were worsening in all areas of American society.

> Politically and socially, America was in some ways close to chaos. The old party system shattered, and a new one struggled to establish itself on the basis of a confusing array of splinter groups. Corruption in high places was rampant. Although a broad middle class was developing, the gap between the rich and poor was wider than ever before. Immigrants arrived in unprecedented numbers, changing the nation's ethnic makeup and fanning anti-foreign sentiment. Urban death rates soared. America's largest city, New York, could boast of its economic and cultural centrality, but it was also crowded, filthy, and infested by rowdy gangs and roving

prostitutes—not to mention the ever-present swine on the streets ... The economy, which had been booming since the '48 gold rush, contracted sharply in late 1854, resulting in widespread unemployment and suffering. Even the weather did not cooperate. The winter of 1854 was one of the most brutal in memory. Frigid temperatures and wicked storms lashed the eastern seaboard, worsening the misery of thousands already stung by want. (Reynolds, 306)

Rather than despair at his nation's growing ills, however, Whitman set out to reconcile them in his poetry. He firmly believed that a verse which celebrated the diversity of America and its far-reaching social vision could hold together a country in distress and motivate its citizens with a new vision of true democracy.

In fact, Whitman's vision of democracy was nurtured during his childhood by his 'freethinking' parents, Walter and Louisa Whitman, who raised their children in an atmosphere of tolerance and open-mindedness. Brought up in a home that observed many Quaker customs, the "gentle demeanor and peaceful spirituality" of his mother was present in Walt; and when combined with the "broad-mindedness" of his father, the two contributed to the cultural, social, and political, awareness that is prevalent in *Leaves of Grass*.

"Having closely observed almost every aspect of American culture for years, Whitman realized that there were, after all, beliefs and tastes that many Americans shared, even in a time of division and confusion," Reynolds writes. Throughout his poetry, Whitman appealed to common American interests—democracy, devotion to family, love of nature and art—and attempted to bridge the gap between the people that politics and societal conventions had created.

"Individualism was easy to come by in the dropout fifties, but no one took so radical a stand on it as Whitman," writes Reynolds.

Whitman was insistent that the growth of *Leaves of Grass*, from the first volume through eight successive editions, identified with the growth of America the country. Just as he felt he had new things to write and say with each edition, so too did America develop and grow throughout the years. In his mind, the growth and expansion of his lifelong literary creation paralleled the growth of the nation.

In his 1876 preface to the sixth edition of *Leaves*, Whitman summarizes his mood as he and his land developed simultaneously:

> I have lived in fresh lands, inchoate, and in a revolutionary age, future-founding. I have felt to identify the points of that age, these lands, in my recitatives ... Within my time the United States have emrg'd from nebulous vagueness and suspense, to full orbic ... Out of that stretch of time ... my Poems too have found genesis.

By the early 1850's, Whitman had totally given up carpentry as a trade and was working as a full-time newspaperman, but he eventually decided to work part-time as a freelance journalist so that he could focus more time and energy on his poetry. He told no one of his intent to write a book of verse, during which time, he was once again living with his family in Brooklyn, and contributing to their financial support. Despite his commitments, however, he apparently did not struggle with his decision to leave full-time newspaper work. "Whitman's transformation into a genius appears effortless. It seemed simply to happen. Whitman himself could offer no explanation. "I just did what I did because I did it—that's the whole secret," he later wrote. (Swerdlow, 119)

While Whitman did not start writing the actual poems that would form the first volume of *Leaves of Grass* until he was around 30 years old, the "long foreground" that Emerson spoke of in his letter of praise to Whitman was in reference to all the experiences he had encountered up to that point in his life. In a sense, Whitman was composing *Leaves* his whole life, jotting lines of verse on paper scraps and then in a notebook, but he only organized his thoughts with the 1855 publication of a thin folio of poems entitled *Leaves of Grass*.

A small book of 83 pages, it contained a ten-page preface and twelve untitled poems of which the introductory poem, later to be named "Song of Myself" is longer than the other 11 works together. This first volume of *Leaves of Grass* was a thin, folio style leather-bound book with marbled end pages and a rich dark green cover with gold leaf letters spelling out *Leaves of Grass*. The lettering is in the form of a rooted grass plant sprouting new growth, perhaps giving the reader a clue to the growth process the volume of poetry will undergo during its nine successive editions. Whitman wanted the first printing of his work to be a memorable and elegant one and as such, this is the only full-size volume; all other editions were smaller, quarto size that grew thicker as the author added new poems.

Anonymously published at his own expense, Whitman did not credit himself as author, only as the person who requested the copyright, perhaps in an attempt to stress the inclusiveness of his poetry. "The absence of an author emphasized Whitman's belief that the voice in *Leaves* is Everyone." (Swerdlow, 119)

Whitman totally oversaw the production of his "wonderful and ponderous book," including the design and layout of the pages; it is believed that he even set some of the type himself. It was created to be like no other poetry book of its day and was described by Whitman himself as "A thoroughly revolutionary formation. Reynolds has described the publication as a "hands-on, old-style artisan publishing, a throwback to the early days when authors had been directly involved in the publishing process."

> Whitman had it printed at the Brooklyn printing shop of James and Andrew Rome, Scottish immigrants he had known since he had run his own printing establishment in the late forties. In the early spring of 1855, he walked daily from his small frame house on Prince Street, where he still lived with his parents and several siblings, to the Romes' redbrick shop on the corner of Cranberry and Fulton, where he sat at a corner table and read the *Tribune* as the leaves of poetry came off the press. On May 15, he filed the book for copyright with the United States Court in the Southern District of New York. (Reynolds, 310)

There were only 795 copies printed; fewer than 150 are known to survive today and each copy was estimated in 1994 to be worth about $40,000. (Swerdlow, 120)

Written by Whitman as a means to reunite the different factions of American society into one voice that celebrated rather than condemned diversity, *Leaves of Grass* presented a new vision of democracy and egalitarianism that lovingly embraced the whole of society. Keeping with his democratic theme, the collection was released around July 4, 1855.

No where was his intended unity more apparent than on the frontspiece of the first volume of his poetry where an engraving of a "lounging working man, broad-hatted, bearded, shirt open at the neck to reveal a colored undershirt, his right arm akimbo, left hand in his pants pocket, [with his] weight on the right leg" greeted readers. (Baym, et. al., 917-18)

The image was of a working man, not one who normally would be associated with reading or writing verse, defying the reader to question his 'right' to be there. It is a clear indication of the innovative and unconventional poetry, both in form and theme, that will follow—celebrating the ordinary and common in everyday life, espousing a new democracy that embraces and unites all and a society where working men could read or write poetry. "The preface, was likewise bold and daring, focusing on the sort of poet he thought America required and the kind of poetry that America could expect from him. 'The American poets are to enclose old and new for America is the race of races. Of them a bard is to be commensurate with a people.'" (Bloom, 13).

The first lines of "Song of Myself," likewise, epitomize that oneness:

.   I celebrate myself, and sing myself
        And what I assume you shall assume,
        For every atom belonging to me as good belongs to you.

This new American poet would develop new forms and subject matter for his poetry where free verse would be prominent and rhyme, if used at all, would not be primary. Meter and stanzaic formation were unimportant. The content of the poems, too, would be altered from the over-sentimentalized verse of the early 1800's to a more deeply genuine style respecting the reality of everyday life.

Whitman fully expected that his poetry would be absorbed by the people of the country whom he believed had so long awaited a true poet of the people. He was sorely disappointed. Bookstores on the whole refused to carry the work because it supported equality between men and women as well as the rich and the poor; Whitman's discussion of the human body likewise made people uncomfortable. His own mother, always one of his staunchest supporters, described the collection as "muddled." His books, many of which were distributed for free to prominent poets of the time, were discarded, and those that were read were largely rejected as "trash."

He did achieve some fame as his style lent itself to parody. In 1857, the London *Examiner* offered its version of a Whitman poem—"The teapot, five coffee cups, sugar basin, and cover, four saucers and six cups"—poking fun at the cataloging and repetition so prominent in "Song of Myself." (Swerdlow, 120)

Detedmined to gain an audience for his work, the stubborn Whitman resorted to writing unsigned reviews praising his work for local newspapers. "An American bard at last!" read one; another proclaimed, "We announce a great Philosopher—perhaps a great poet." (120)

Despite the lukewarm public response, Emerson hailed *Leaves of Grass* as "the most extraordinary piece of wit and wisdom America has yet contributed" and his letter to Whitman buoyed his spirit and encouraged him in his poetic mission.

Shortly after the publication of *Leaves*, Whitman's father passed away, and Whitman assumed full financial responsibility for his mother and a mentally challenged brother. He continued with some freelance newspaper work to meet his commitments, but Whitman's true passion lay in writing his poetry. By July of 1856, Whitman had written twenty more poems, some of his most powerful and moving, and was set to publish a second edition of *Leaves of Grass*.

The 1856 volume was striking in its presentation of Whitman's work as an actual book of poetry, with 32 poems, all titled and presented in a table of contents. The 384-page volume was quarto size, designed by Whitman "to be carried in the pocket" of readers and was priced at $1 a copy, well within the common man's reach.

Perhaps the most remarkable thing about this second edition, however, was the exploitation of Emerson's letter of praise for the first volume of *Leaves of Grass*. Not only did Whitman reprint it in full in the 1856 edition, citing "I greet you at the beginning of a great career" emblazoned in gold on the book's spine, but he also wrote and published a reply to his "dear friend and master" and presented the 32 poems (12 originals and 20 new poems) as a "gift" to Emerson. This "brash gimmick" bestowed Emerson's praise on twenty poems that he had never seen. (Reynolds, 355)

This reprinting of Emerson's letter was designed to attract more attention and readers to the second volume of *Leaves of Grass* and was in keeping with Whitman's bombastic personality, for Whitman was "an egotist without parallel," who "wanted all the world to see what a truly great man thought of him" (Leipold, 61)

Despite the abject failure of the first volume of *Leaves of Grass* and the moderate success of volume two, Whitman now envisioned himself more as a poet than as a newspaperman and spent a great deal of time socializing with other artists with whom he could have literary and creative discussions. By the mid-to-late 1850's, Whitman had become a legend of sorts in the bohemian community of New York City, frequenting a downtown restaurant and saloon named Pfaff's located on Broadway in today's SoHo area:

> It was the favorite haunt of New York City's unconventional. All types of visionaries including writers, actors, socialites, painters and musicians flocked to Pfaff's basement to eat and drink a climate that encouraged noisy debate. A published author and the target of moral outrage from more established society, Whitman was somewhat of a local celebrity at Pfaff's. His fellow artists celebrated him as a literary rebel and a hero of free expression. (Whitman Interpretive Center)

Whitman enjoyed the attention and notoriety he received at Pfaff's, sometimes reciting poetry but mostly just sitting and listening to the noise around him. "My favorite pleasure at Pfaff's," he later explained, "was to look on, to see, to talk little and to absorb." (Whitman Interpretive Center)

From 1856 through 1860, Whitman continued to write poetry, visit Pfaff's for literary inspiration and frequent working-class neighborhoods "seeking to know the common man better through direct association with him."

> Hours would be spent along the docks, visiting with longshoremen and sailors ... riding with draymen on their horse-drawn wagons; on other occasions a bus was his conveyance, once driving the horse himself when the regular busman was ill. He was 'gathering atmosphere,' and he went to the common people to get it. (Leipold, 60)

By 1857, Whitman's responsibility for his family and the less than stellar commercial success of the first two editions of *Leaves of Grass* caused recurring financial difficulties, and he was required to take day work as editor at the *Brooklyn Times*. For the next two years, through 1859, Whitman wrote numerous editorials regarding the national discussion on slavery, all the while he continued to work on his poetry. Reporting by day and writing poetry by night, Whitman was poised to release a third edition of *Leaves of Grass* by 1860, which included his most personal series of poems to date.

Of those published, 146 new poems entitled "Calamus" and "Children of Adam" were very sexually explicit, apparently expressing Whitman's repressed homosexual longings and his torment over how to deal with those sexual urges. "Expressing physical love of both men and women and dealing candidly with human sexuality, these poems intensified the public's outrage against Whitman. Even his own most liberal ally, Emerson, had urged the poet towards self-censorship." (Whitman Interpretive Center) Whitman, however, always the egotist and individualist refused, writing "I felt down in my soul the clear and unmistakable conviction to disobey all and to pursue my own way."

This period of Whitman's life was a time of torment spent dealing with his sexual identity and handling what had become a sordid family life:

> His brother Andrew's widow became a prostitute and neglected her children; an older sister was embittered by marriage to an unsuccessful artist; a brother crazed by syphilis had violent spells in which he threatened their mother; a feeble-minded brother shared a room with Whitman; and his mother, always idealized in Whitman's poems and his recollections, seems to have been a whining, self-pitying nag. (Baym, et. al., 3rd edition, 1956)

Late in 1860, however, Whitman's luck turned for the better with a letter he received from the young and enthusiastic Boston publishing firm of Thayer and Eldridge, who asked permission to publish the third edition of *Leaves of Grass*.

"We are young men. We 'celebrate' ourselves by acts. Try us. You can do us good. We can do you good—pecuniarily." (Baym, et. al., 919)

For the first time in his writing career, at the age of 41, Walt Whitman had a publisher. The response to this third edition of *Leaves of Grass* was a mixed bag. While public response was generally positive, the sexual content continued to create problems for many of Whitman's readers and literary counterparts alike. While in Boston overseeing the publication of his collection, Emerson attempted to introduce Whitman to the Boston literary circle amid objections from more conventional poets such as Longfellow, Holmes and Lowell; likewise the families of Emerson, Thoreau, and Alcott all refused his company at their homes in Concord, Massachusetts.

Later that year, in October 1860, Whitman was dealt another blow with the bankruptcy filing of his publisher, Thayer and Eldridge. Despite the fact that this had nothing to do with their publication of *Leaves*, royalties from his collection were not forthcoming and Whitman received the meager sum of $250 for his entire publication. In addition, publication of the edition was stopped and the multitude of copies Whitman had hoped to circulate became an impossibility.

WHITMAN THE WOUND DRESSER

April 13, 1861 was a warm balmy night, unusual for this time of year in New York City. Walt Whitman had just exited an opera on Broadway and was wandering down the street, near his beloved Pfaff's Restaurant, when excited newsboys announced the Confederate attack on Fort Sumter signaling the beginning of the Civil War.

Since 1855 when his first collection of untitled poems was released in a beautifully bound, green leather portfolio entitled *Leaves of Grass*, Walt Whitman had become a regular on the New York City scene, frequenting the opera as well as the docks and working-class pubs, looking for inspiration for his ever growing poetry portfolio.

Whitman was an enigma to many, a keen observer of life who recorded his feelings and observations in his unconventional and controversial 19th-century poetry. Much of his writing dealt with the notion of equality and democracy in all areas of society such as education and industry. He strongly believed that disenfranchised individuals of society, particularly women and slaves, were entitled to freedoms often given only to white male citizens.

Whitman, however, was also a man of his times:

Reflecting the prejudices of contemporary science and popular thought, he believed blacks and whites were not innately equal and his views on race were frequently contradictory; and his opinion often violated the radically egalitarian views expressed in his poetry. Despite these beliefs, he declared himself the poet of all people saying "I am the poet of slaves and of the master of slaves." (Whitman Interpretive Center)

Despite these beliefs he felt the institution of slavery, in particular, was against the very ideals of true democracy that he espoused in his writings and he advocated the resolution of the issue through peaceful compromise. Privately, Whitman, like most Americans, feared that a war of disunion over the issue of slavery would greatly damage the country and he argued publicly against the use of war to settle the issue.

Like President Abraham Lincoln, however, Whitman felt that the issue of slavery, while a reprehensible institution, was secondary to the preservation of the Union.

Thus, when the Civil War erupted that spring-like night in April, 1861, Whitman fully committed himself to the Union cause and remained a powerful and passionate supporter of President Lincoln for the duration of the conflict.

Anxious to keep the public informed about the ravages of the war, Whitman drew on his extensive journalistic experience and moved from his longtime home of New York state to Washington, D.C. in the fall of 1861. His time spent on the battlefields of the war between the states marked a turning point in Walt Whitman's life and acted as a catalyst that reinvigorated his life and artistic purpose.

Visiting the front, attending to amputees, meeting black Union soldiers, walking through prison camps and forgoing the "fat meats and late suppers" he had grown accustomed to in New York City, Whitman gathered information for his compassionate and comprehensive war reports. In the articles he wrote, Northern readers were given detailed eyewitness accounts of the damages and human horrors that the war was leveling upon their sons, brothers, husbands and, fathers serving their country hundreds of miles from home.

"The merit of these war pieces, is not strictly literary," Whitman later wrote. "If they have merit, it is chiefly human."

The travesty of war took a more personal turn in December, 1862. Since the war was taking place primarily in the South, news was often slow in getting to the families in the North. To keep loved ones informed, local newspapers periodically ran lists of soldiers who had been wounded or killed in battle. One day, while perusing the paper, Whitman came upon the name of a "George Whitman," an officer in the 51st regiment from New York, who had been injured in Virginia. While he was uncertain if this "George Whitman" was his brother or not, Whitman knew George was serving with the New York regiment and he quickly prepared to leave New York City and travel to the frontlines of the Civil War to determine if the injured soldier was his younger brother. Although he had not always maintained close connections with his siblings,—"Being a blood brother to a man," he said, "Don't make him a real brother" (Swerdlow, 136)—Whitman's sense of loyalty and concern for his mother's feelings, however, overtook him and he retraced his brother George's service route and indeed discovered him in a Union camp overlooking Fredericksburg, where he apparently had been stationed and was wounded.

Thankfully, George's injury was only a superficial face wound from which he quickly recovered. However, the effect of the journey to the Union camp had on Walt Whitman left permanent scars on the poet's psyche and changed him forever. He had fallen into a rut of sorts in New York, writing some sentimental pieces and poems for local papers and eating and drinking his way through the downtown pubs. He was stagnant both personally and professionally, and the journey to find George ultimately served a two-fold purpose: to reunite his family and to reinvigorate his art.

In his essay, "The Wound Dresser," author Paul Zweig describes Whitman's war experiences that renewed and redirected the poet's artistic purpose:

> Whitman's notebook reflects his state of mind. He has been pulled out of his "slough"—out of himself—by the grim scenes of the later battle and by the soldiers: young men like his New York stage drivers and ferryboatmen, made lean and curiously hearty the experiences of the war. He walks along

the Rappahannock River and sees Fredericksburg, "splintered, bursted, crumbled, the houses—some with their chimney thrown down—the hospitals—the man with his mouth blown out." on a bright, freezing day, he [Whitman] admires a regimental inspection, the men "sifted by death, dismemberment, etc. from eleven hundred men (including recruits) to about two hundred." He sits around fireplaces improvised in holes in the ground, and is stirred by the "brightly beautiful" scene of wagon trains, encampments, locomotives, and stacked rifles, spread out over miles of battlefield. Everywhere there are graves; bodies on stretchers, covered with brown and gray blankets. (Zweig, 144)

The sights and sounds of his journey through the war zone, horrendous though they were, provided Whitman with new fodder for a remarkable collection of poems about the devastation of the war that would eventually form "Drum Taps."

In "A Sight in Camp in the Daybreak Gray and Dim," a poem included in "Drum Taps," Whitman describes to the reader what confronts him upon leaving his tent one morning:

> A sight in camp in the daybreak gray and dim,
> As from my tent I emerge so early sleepless,
> As slow I walk in the cool fresh air the path near by the hospital
>   tent,
> Three forms I see on stretchers lying, brought out there untended
>   lying,
> Over each the blanket spread, ample brownish woolen blanket,
> Gray and heavy blanket, folding, covering all.
>
> Curious I halt and silent stand,
> Then with light fingers I from the face of the nearest the first just
>   lift the blanket;
> Who are you elderly man so gaunt and grim, with well-gray'd
>   hair and flesh all sunken about the eyes?
> Who are you my dear comrade?

Then to the second I step—and who are you my child and
    darling?
Who are you sweet boy with cheeks yet blooming?

Then to the third—a face nor child nor old, very calm, as of
    beautiful yellow-white ivory
Young man I think I know you—I think this face is the face
    of the Christ himself,
Dead and divine and brother of all, and here again he lies.

Whitman committed himself to serve the wounded and dying
soldiers that flooded Washington's war hospitals despite the fact that he
had no money, nowhere to stay and no official purpose there. Life in
New York seemed a distant memory to him; his concerns there almost
silly by comparison.

"Now that I have lived for 8 or 9 days amid such scenes as the
camps furnish," he wrote his mother, "... really nothing we call trouble
seems worth talking about."

Determined somehow to stay in Washington, Whitman wrote to
Ralph Waldo Emerson asking for assistance in finding some work in
Washington to cover his expenses:

> Dear Friend,
> Breaking up a few weeks since, and for good, my New
> York stagnation—wandering since through camp and battle
> scenes—I fetch up here in harsh and superb plight—
> wretchedly poor, excellent well, (my only torment, family
> matters)—realizing at last that it is necessary for me to fall
> for the time in the wise olds way, to push my fortune, to be
> brazen, and get employment, and have an income—
> determined to do it, (at any rate until I get out of horrible
> slough).

Whether his letter to Emerson was effective or not is unclear;
however, within several days, Whitman had indeed landed a job as a
copyist for an army paymaster named Major Hapgood. Whitman's good
friend and former publisher, William Eldridge, of the now defunct
Thayer and Eldridge, publisher of the third edition of *Leaves of Grass*,

worked in the Army Paymaster's office and it is believed that he facilitated Walt's hiring. Now, with a part-time income and a "weary little bedroom" in a roominghouse on L Street in Washington, Whitman's days were spent between mornings working for the Major and afternoons visiting "poor sick pale tattered soldiers" in the close to 30 army hospitals that existed in and around Washington, D.C.

Black or white, Union or Confederate—it made no difference to Whitman. The poet who had long seen himself as the "Good Grey Poet of Long Island" was beginning to see himself as a voice for *all* Americans. His ability to comfort and ease the pain of others was a gift to the soldiers and cultivated for Walt "the dear work of comrades" that was to fill his wartime poetry. Meager though his own existence was, Whitman never visited the hospitals without little treats for the soldiers—a newspaper, peppermints, peaches, brandy, writing paper, fruit juices, small amounts of tobacco—anything, to bring a moment's worth of joy into these suffering young mens' lives.

Whitman became completely immersed in the war effort; no longer was he on the outside of the war looking in. The role of observer quietly and suddenly disappeared and the role of minister to the sick emerged. Whitman absorbed all the suffering, loneliness and devastation he had experienced while traveling through the camps and visiting hospital wards.

His priorities were evident in a letter he wrote to his brother, Jeff, in April 1863:

> It doesn't seem to me it makes so much difference about worldly successes, (beyond just enough to eat and drink, and shelter, in the moderatest limits) anymore, since the last four months of my life especially, and that merely to *live*, and have one fair meal a day, is *enough*. (Zweig, 149)

His brother raised money throughout the war from his coworkers at the Brooklyn Water Works and sent it to Whitman to buy little gifts for the soldiers he visited at the hospitals.

All the while, the great observer of life, the journalist and the poet kept notes and recorded daily in a little book, details about each and every soldier he met. Whitman's intent was to write a book, bearing the Civil War's soul for all Americans to see.

In his essay entitled "The Wound Dresser," author Paul Zweig writes that Whitman intended to "give America a view of her own suffering soul; he would make the invisible visible: the hospitals, those forgotten places where the debris of the war had been cast up—a debris of living young men suffering from the grotesque wounds of war. A boy with a pierced bladder dribbles urine through his wound. Another boy gives off a smell of rot from a gangrenous leg. Another, dying of a stomach wound, looks untouched and peaceful, sleeping the sleep of youth that degenerates day by day into a fever-ridden anguish and then death."

Whitman's reminiscings, entitled *Memoranda during the War*, were rejected for publication by his Boston friend James Redpath and only made it into print a decade or so later as a part of *Specimen Days*. Like the first edition of *Leaves of Grass*, Walt Whitman published this himself.

By his own account, Whitman had made over 600 hospital visits and sat with close to 100,000 soldiers by the war's end. So deep was the impression he left on these ailing soldiers that for many years after the war was over, Whitman maintained close correspondences with some of the soldiers to whom he ministered during the war of secession. One day, Whitman received a letter in the mail from a young man he had faithfully visited in the Washington, D.C. hospital during his convalescence. Announcing the birth of his son, the soldier lovingly told Whitman that the boy, Walter Whitman, had been named after the man who read to him and kept him company during the darkest days of his life.

The note read: "We have had a son born, and we call him Walter Whitman in honor of you, for the love of you." (Whitman Interpretive Center)

The poet of democracy who had praised the strength and unity of his nation throughout the first three editions of *Leaves of Grass* became an eyewitness to the horrors that democracy exacted on our nation. His Civil War experiences served not to destroy his beliefs of freedom and democracy but to further strengthen his commitment to one country, united in its struggles and successes.

Despite the devastation and destruction the country endured during the war, Whitman's sense of the goodness and fortitude of the American people remained unwavering and constant. He truly became the "Quintessential American Poet," one who acknowledged in his writings both the darkest days and brightest hours of what it meant to be an American.

WHITMAN LOOKS TOWARDS THE FUTURE

During the years of the Civil War, Walt Whitman totally immersed himself in tending to the wounded and dying soldiers and recorded many of his thoughts and feelings into a notebook he carried around with him from hospital to hospital. These men, many of them boys as young as 15 and far from home, grew attached to Whitman and the emotional demands on him were great.

"The men," he wrote his mother, "hunger and thirst for attention; this is sometimes the only thing that will reach their condition." (Swerdlow, 136). He exerted so much emotional energy to his hospital visits that he soon began to suffer physical side effects such as sleeplessness, dizziness, and severe headaches. The already barrel-chested, 180 pound Whitman ballooned to over 215 pounds quickly and experienced severe writer's block, unable to compose anything for a period of time.

Washington, D.C. in 1863 when Whitman arrived was a study in contrasts, both "dazzling and depressing" at the same time. (Reynolds, 421) The beautiful edifices such as the Capitol and other government buildings stood side by side with the squalor in the unpaved streets. For Whitman, however, it was the embodiment of the full range of American culture—common everyday events such as herding thousands of cattle through the streets existed simultaneously with the majesty of government. Almost one hundred forts were erected to ward off General Lee's approaching troops, yet men still worked, women still gave birth and life went on.

Whitman reveled in this display of truly American conditions— the grandeur of a government guiding a united people, yet the devastation of a nation warding off disunion. While he spent most of his free time compassionately serving the wounded in the D.C. hospitals, Whitman eventually was able to write again, feeling this period of history should not go unreported. He tried his hand at writing a prose piece that brought to life for readers the daily horrors of the fighting men.

Drum Taps, published in October, 1865 contained fifty-three poems presented in a thin, black covered book. It represented a subtle yet sure change in Whitman's writing style, the poems of which "conformed more obviously to mainstream expectations than had any of the poems in *'Leaves of Grass,'*" according to author Reynolds. It was a collection of prose-poetry that incorporated some standard stanza and rhythm conventions, and in doing so, brought more positive praise for Whitman's writing ability than any of his previous journalistic or poetry endeavors.

While established writers like Henry James and William Dean Howells who were unaccustomed to Whitman's new writing style found the volume "disagreeable," other literary figures saw merit in Whitman's offerings. Gay Wilson Allen, noted Whitman biographer, believes that the review by John Burroughs, "Walt Whitman and his 'Drum Taps,'" which appeared in the New York *Galaxy* in October, 1866 "provided the first detailed appreciation of Whitman ['s work.]" (Reynolds, 459).

Burroughs, a Washington friend of Whitman's wrote:

> He has been sneered at and mocked and ridiculed, he has been cursed and caricatured and persecuted, and instead of retorting in a like strain, or growing embittered or misanthropic he has preserved his serenity and good nature under all ... his [Whitman's] poetry means power, health, freedom, democracy, self-esteem, a full life in the open air, an escape from old forms and standards. (Reynolds, 459)

The *Drum Taps* collection included poems in which the mournfulness and shock of the ravages of the war were alternated with unwavering support for the preservation of the Union and the hope that one day the country would again be united. Whitman was hopeful for its future and remained convinced of the goodness and fortitude of the American people as embodied in the stoic and dignified way their sons and husbands served and died for their country.

In the poem "The Wound Dresser," Whitman described his daily duties on the hospital floor:

On, on I go, (open doors of time! open hospital doors!)
The crush'd head I dress, (poor crazed hand tear not the bandage
    away,)
The neck of the cavalry-man with the bullet through and through
    I examine,

Hard the breathing rattles, quite glazed already the eye, yet life
   struggles hard,
(Come sweet death! be persuaded O beautiful death! In mercy
   come quickly.)

From the stump of the arm, the amputated hand,
I undo the clotted lint, remove the slough, wash off the matter and
   blood,
Back on his pillow, the soldier bends with curv'd neck and side-
   falling head,
His eyes are closed, his face is pale, he dares not look on the
   bloody stump,
And has not yet look'd on it.

Despite the graphic war descriptions, the *Drum Taps* collection,
now with a "sequel" added, ended on a hopeful note. In 1865, with the
war over, the country was reconstructing and the poet extolled the
promise of the America to come. In "Turn O Libertad," Whitman
focused on the future, challenging his readers to leave the past behind:

Turn O Libertad, for the war is over
From it and all henceforth expanding, doubting no more, resolute,
         sweeping the world
Turn from lands retrospective recording proofs of the past,
From the singers that sing the trailing glories ...
then turn, and be not alarm'd O Libertad—turn your undying
         face,
To where the future, greater than all the past,
Is swiftly, surely preparing for you.

One of Whitman's most memorable experiences while living in
Washington, was his presence at the second inauguration ball of
President Abraham Lincoln, a man he had long admired but never met.
In fact, years before Lincoln was elected to a first term in 1861, Whitman
had written a poem reflecting his hope for the ascent of a "Redeemer
President" from "the real West, the log hut, the clearing, the woods, the
prairie." (Swerdlow, 137) Never a staunch supporter of organized
politics, Whitman found in Lincoln a politician and leader whom he

believed embodied and shared his own egalitarian view of democracy. When tensions escalated towards war in the 1850's, Whitman argued against it to settle the disagreement, believing slavery was an institution whose days were naturally numbered. However, when war began, Whitman fervently supported President Lincoln calling him "The greatest, best, most characteristic, artistic, moral personality" in the country.

After the war was over, Whitman stopped his visits to the hospitals, possibly suffering from something akin to today's post-traumatic stress syndrome. As Swrdlow suggests, "His sleeplessness and distress resembled what is now called post-traumatic stress disorder. He was 46 years old, and looked like an old man. 'I would try to write, blind, blind, with my own tears,' Whitman later said." (Swerdlow, 138)

He continued to rework *Leaves of Grass*, incorporating "Drum Taps," "Sequel," and 6 new poems into the fourth edition, released in 1867. Still a shameless self-promoter, Whitman wrote more anonymous reviews of this latest edition, hoping once again for the recognition and monetary rewards that accompany acceptance. However, the latest edition was the most disorganized and "chaotically arranged" version of *Leaves of Grass* yet to be released. Critics believe that the mental depression Walt Whitman endured following his years of being so close to the action of the war are reflected in the disorder in this edition. "My book and the war are one," he later wrote as he came to understand the effect the war had on his writing. (Whitman Interpretive Center)

In 1865, Whitman was working in the Bureau of Indian Affairs at the Department of the Interior, having decided to stay in Washington during the Reconstruction Period. Never far from his poetry, however, Whitman kept a copy of the latest edition of *Leaves of Grass* in his top desk drawer wrapped in a blue book to hide its cover from view. Still not a widely read work by average citizens, Whitman was unknown to many as the author of this controversial work. When James Harlan, then Secretary of the Interior and Whitman's superior, discovered that he was the author of that "scandalous and indecent work" Whitman was fired immediately. Today's expression referring to pornography as "blue book" material has its origins in this incident.

He was quickly placed in another position in the Attorney General's office but the indignation of his friends after his firing resulted in the publication of a work by Whitman's friend and abolitionist novelist, William Douglas O'Connor, defending the poet's genius and reputation. Entitled "The Good Grey Poet," a name that quickly became a term of endearment for Whitman, O'Connor's piece set off a series of complimentary reviews of Whitman and contributed to a steadily growing reputation both here and overseas.

Shortly after this, another dear friend, naturalist John Burroughs, published a biography of Whitman, called "Notes of Walt Whitman as a Poet and a Person."

During this period, the United States was slowly entering an era of reconstruction and industrial growth following many years of wartime destruction. Whitman was encouraged by the technological advances that were being made and the new poems in the fifth edition of *Leaves of Grass*, released in 1871-1872, reflected his optimism for the modern age. The title poem of this latest edition, "A Passage to India," applauds the incredible feats of engineering that promised to improve worldwide communication such as the TransContinental Railroad, the Suez Canal and the TransAtlantic Telegraph.

He writes:

Singing my days,
Singing the great achievements of the present,
Singing the strong light works of engineers,
Our modern wonders, (the antique ponderous Seven outvied,)
In the Old World the east the Suez canal,
The New by its mighty railroad spann'd,
The seas inlaid with eloquent gentle wires;
Yet first to sound, and ever sound, the cry with thee O soul,
The Past! the Past! the Past!

As optimistic as he was about such progress, however, Whitman was equally as distressed by the corruption and greed he saw growing in American government. He had hoped that the Civil War would eradicate these demoralizing and immoral activities and instead create a new sense of democracy based on honesty, dignity and integrity where all citizens had equal opportunity. The opposite occurred, however, as the division between the wealthy class and the poor grew even greater; Whitman watched, horrified, as postwar America slipped deeper into moral decay.

In his 1871 essay, "Democratic Vistas," Whitman wrote that "genuine belief seems to have left us. The underlying principles of the states are not honestly believed in nor is humanity itself believed in." This essay, one of Whitman's most piercing social commentaries, shows how his disillusionment with certain aspects of American democracy colored his view of society as a whole. (Whitman Interpretive Center)

His unsettled mood was also reflected in revisions he made to the 5th edition of *Leaves of Grass* such as the lines he added to his poem of social protest "Respondez!":

"Stifled those days, o lands, in every public and private corruption.
Smother in thievery, impotence, shamelessness mountain high."

No where is Whitman's state of mind during the early to mid-1870's more succinctly captured than at the Walt Whitman Interpretive Center at his birthplace in West Hills, Long Island, New York:

While America was experiencing rapid and remarkable industrial growth, Walt Whitman saw the soul of his country dying. The wonders of the individual, celebrated by Whitman, were being crushed in the roaring factories and overcrowded cities of post-war America. The government was corrupt, he felt, and no longer to be trusted. Even the people, victims of the country's worsening conditions had become 'ungrammatical, untidy and ill-bred.' For Walt Whitman, part of the blame lay in the shortcomings of American literature that never recognized the people and only produced critical and querulous men. His solution to the problem was the creation of a new literature that would nurture a nation of supple and athletic minds, capable of saving American society.

As he approached the end of his life, however, Walt realized that his dream of a radically new democracy would not occur in his lifetime. This America was far different than the America of his youth.

THE AGING POET

It was during this time period that Whitman, who never married but is rumored to have fathered several illegitimate children, entered into a close friendships with several acquaintances both male and female, the nature of which we will never fully understand. While all his writings espoused celebrating the individual and certain pieces of his poetry touched on heterosexual and homosexual love, history is not definitively clear on Whitman's own sexual orientation. Indeed, many argue that Whitman himself was not clear on his own preferences, and that confusion caused him much mental anguish towards the end of his life. One thing, however, is certain. Whether a love relationship with a woman or a strong friendship with a man, Whitman was capable of feeling and caring very deeply.

Whitman's ability to feel deeply and passionately for someone is embodied in his relationship with Peter Doyle, a young street car driver Whitman met while riding the Washington and Georgetown Railroad one evening just after the war was over in 1865. Whitman was 46 years old; Doyle 18. As is true with most of his relationships, the nature of this particular friendship is unclear; however, the two connected instantly. In his book, *Walt Whitman's America: A Cultural Biography*, author David Reynolds describes their first meeting in Doyle's own words: "We were familiar at once—I put my hand on his knee—we understood ... From that time on we were the biggest sort of friends." (Reynolds, 487) The two were almost inseparable during the early 1870's, usually taking "daily walks out the well-paved military roads towards Alexandria, with Walt singing tunes and reciting poetry, usually Shakespeare. Walt sometimes gave Pete a bouquet or had clothes made for him, and when he went on trips sent him newsy, affectionate letters." (487).

Reynolds writes that the culture of the times "widely accepted intense same-sex passion" so that "he [Whitman] could kiss or spend the night with Doyle openly and without guilt." Whitman, however, was cautious in all his relationships, whether with males or females, to maintain a balance between his sexuality and the wholesomeness of spirit he wrote about in *Leaves of Grass*. This balancing act preoccupied Whitman throughout his later years and he continued to struggle with his sexual persuasion through notebook jottings for the rest of his life.

The most intense relationship with a woman appears to have been with an Englishwoman named Anne Gilchrist, a widow with three children, who fell for Whitman after reading the Rossetti (1869) edition of *Leaves of Grass*. Moved by the content of his poems, in particular the "Children of Adam" pieces, Gilchrist wrote to Whitman in 1871 relating her emotions upon reading his writings:

> It was the divine soul embracing mine. I never before dreamed what love was like; nor what life meant. Never was alive before. No words but 'new birth' can hint the meaning of what then happened to me. (Reynolds, 491-92)

Whitman continued to write Gilchrist who became so enamored of the poet that she offered to bear him children. Sensing the evolution of a relationship he wasn't interested in, Whitman continued to correspond with her via letter, eventually gently squashing hope on her part of anything more than a friendship. The two maintained contact until Gilchrist moved back to England with her family in 1879.

The year 1873 was a pivotal one for Whitman and marked the beginning of the decline of his physical health. In January of that year, he suffered the first of several strokes he was to experience and was partially paralyzed as a result. At the age of 53, he was forced to leave his beloved Washington and move in with his brother, George and his wife, Louisa to a rowhome in Camden, New Jersey during his convalescence. His brother, a pipe fitter in a Camden tool shop was well-meaning and attentive; however, he was not able to provide Whitman with the intellectual stimulation he had in D.C. or with the emotional support he garnered from his relationship with Peter Doyle. To compound his sorrows, Whitman's mother, with whom he had remained very close, died that same year. Although he could still write and frequently did, Whitman slipped into what he would call "the worst, darkest, doubtfullest period of my life" prompted as much by his physical debilitation as by his distancing from Doyle. Once Whitman moved to Camden, the two never saw each other again. (Whitman Interpretive Center)

Despite his depression and physical handicaps, Whitman continued to work and found the strength to compile a new edition of *Leaves of Grass* in honor of the country's centennial in 1876. The sixth edition of *Leaves* was a reissue of the 1871-1872 fifth edition and included a second volume, entitled "Two Rivulets" which was a new arrangement of previously published poetry and prose pieces. The physical arrangement of this edition graphically depicted Whitman's hope, as outlined in his Preface, that the new volume "would embody two altogether distinct veins or strata; politics were one and for the other, the pensive thought of immortality."

This dualism, discussing politics for the centennial event and immortality from an aging poet's point of view, are clearly evident in the physical set up of this edition. His newest poems, "Centennial Songs," were placed on the top half of each page with his social and political musings, entitled "Thought on the Centennial," occupying the bottom half of each page.

Still living in Camden with his family, Whitman's financial condition was dire; his lifelong efforts of writing only earned him a few thousand dollars and by 1876, the poet was poverty-stricken. On the heels of the 1876 Centennial edition of *Leaves of Grass*, legislation was introduced into the United States Congress requesting financial support for Whitman, noting his literary contributions and his current state of neglect. It did not pass, however, and Whitman was forced to rely for income on the kindness of his friends and admirers.

Despite the fact that he never felt fully absorbed by his own countrymen, for years Whitman had been embraced by an overseas audience. The author who hoped that his lifelong work, *Leaves of Grass*, would promote love and solidarity among people not only in the United States but around the world, was championed by literary legends such as Alfred Lord Tennyson, Oscar Wilde and Bram Stoker as well as prominent literary critics such as William Michael Rossetti. Collections were often taken up among his overseas admirers and the funds were sent to the debilitated poet.

His most ardent group of devotees, however, was a small band of workingmen in Northern England who in the 1880's formed a weekly Whitman reading and discussion group which they called the Eagle Street College. Elated that his works were being discussed seriously by working people, the poet became deeply attached to this group in his later years, often writing to them daily. The College sent Whitman gifts of money on his birthday each year. In appreciation, Whitman sent the group a lock of his hair and his stuffed canary—his former pet and the subject of his poem, "My Canary Bird." (Whitman Interpretive Center)

For most of his writing career, Whitman's works were vilified for "alleged obscenity" by puritanical America, however with the publication of "Democratic Vistas" (1871) and "Memories of President Lincoln" (1865) some critics began to see Whitman's writings in a different light and his reputation, which had already been established overseas, steadily grew in America.

By 1881, Whitman had put the finishing touches on a seventh edition of *Leaves of Grass* and was well enough to travel to Boston to oversee the production of this latest volume of his work. Both Whitman and his publisher, James Osgood, were confident that this was the edition that would bring him both fame and fortune. However, upon publication on March 1, 1882, the Boston District Attorney's Office immediately started proceedings to have the book banned. Osgood quickly encouraged Whitman to delete the sections deemed indecent and reissue the book; Whitman declined and turned over publication of the volume to David McKay of Philadelphia. Finally, at this late stage of life, Whitman had found a publisher who was devoted and dedicated to his writings. McKay and Whitman remained friends for the rest of Whitman's life. Ironically, the threat of legal action by the District Attorney's Office resulted in a large interest in this volume, which contained 20 new poems, and Whitman received his largest amount of royalties ever from this edition.

WHITMAN'S TWILIGHT YEARS

The later years for Walt Whitman were a time of great contrasts. The poet who had spent all his life writing for and about the American people had gone largely unnoticed, or at least unrespected by the majority of them. Now, as he approached his seventies, his work was beginning to generate discussion and finally, he was earning some money.

The bard, who had long celebrated heartiness of mind and body was failing physically and becoming more and more dependent on the financial support of his close group of friends.

The man who most strongly identified with the working class of America was now befriended by international poets such as Alfred Lord Tennyson and Oscar Wilde and was painted by renowned artists George

W. Waters, John White Alexander, and Thomas Eakins. He was also sculpted by Sidney Morse.

The prophet who had worked tirelessly throughout his life to gain an audience for his work was now surrounded, almost constantly, by friends and followers who interviewed him and took down every word he uttered. Horace Traubel, a longtime confidant, spent over two years faithfully recording his conversations with Whitman during this period. His record, *With Walt Whitman in Camden*, ran to over a million words.

The elderly Whitman continued to express his optimism for a bright American future through his poetry, essays and interviews. The idealized society he wrote of in *Leaves of Grass*, however, was still far off. The young poet who had confidently proclaimed "I am the bard of the future" finally accepted that this era lay beyond his life span. While he never received the national recognition that he craved during his lifetime, Whitman took great comfort knowing that his "audience would lay in the future."

Old age and poor health seemed to liberate Whitman from these lifelong and lofty pursuits and his final days spent in Camden were by all reports a peaceful time when "he could still write and did; and he could enjoy his friendships in leisure, along with the natural world which ... he enjoy[ed] with delicious serenity." (Van Doren, xvi)

In late 1883, Whitman's brother George and his wife decided to move from Camden to a farm in nearby Burlington County, New Jersey and asked Walt to accompany them. Whitman, who had managed to put away some of the meager royalties he received from his works, declined and looked for a house of his own.

In March 1884, he bought his first and only home at 328 Mickle Street in Camden for $1,750 ($1,250 from royalties and a $500 loan from his wealthy friend George W. Childs). It was here that Whitman entertained literary visitors and spent the remaining days of his life.

A brown frame house with two rooms on each of the two floors, Whitman lived here for eight years with his housekeeper Mrs. Davis, who worked for him for free rent and board. Quite an animal enthusiast, Davis turned the house into a "petting zoo" of sorts according to David Reynolds in *Walt Whitman's America: A Cultural Biography*. She also decorated the home with some of her own memorabilia, much from seaside visits which brought joy to the old poet who as a young boy had spent so much time frolicking on the beach in Long Island.

Reynolds writes:

After she moved in, the house became a kind of combined dime museum and petting zoo. An animal lover, Mrs. Davis brought with her a cat, a dog, two turtledoves, a canary, a robin she had saved from a cat, and some hens she kept in an outhouse in the backyard. 'We need but a snake—then our menagerie will be complete,' Whitman once joked. Along with her pets and furniture, she brought along memorabilia like shells and curiosities from all over the world, including a model ship which she hung in the front parlor much to Whitman's pleasure. (548)

In many ways, the Mickle Street house was very similar in disposition to the first house Whitman lived in with his family in Brooklyn. Located near the train tracks and on a street busy with neighborhood children playing and men going to work in the nearby factories, it was noisy and "quite a musical study" for the aging poet. He also enjoyed listening to the whistling at a nearby shipyard.

Whitman 's house had a beautiful tree out front where he would sit for hours in good weather and a grape vine and fruit and flowering trees in the back. Despite its urban location, Whitman's home had a rural feel. Even though it was located in an industrial area that often smelled of factory discharge, the Mickle Street house was the perfect combination of activity and peaceful respite for Whitman.

Ever since his first stroke in 1873, Whitman had been plagued by health problems which contributed to his growing financial difficulties. By the mid-1880's he was no longer able to support himself and his close friends solicited funds to assist Whitman.

At his Birthplace, the drive to support Whitman is concisely outlined: "One of the most successful schemes was concocted by Thomas Donaldson in 1885, a Philadelphia lawyer, who sent letters out to 36 of America's most prominent cultural figures asking them each for a $10 donation to help buy a horse and buggy for the greatly debilitated Whitman." The response was nearly unanimous.

Mark Twain, whose book *Huckleberry Finn* had recently received the same sting from Boston censors that *Leaves of Grass* had received three years earlier, responded immediately, expressing 'great veneration for the old man.'

Nationally acclaimed poet, John Greenleaf Whittier, who was believed to have thrown his complimentary copy of *Leaves of Grass* into the fireplace, sent his donation with a tart comment that hopefully Walt Whitman's new horse 'would be more serviceable to him than the untamed rough jolting Pegasus that he has been accustomed to riding.' (Whitman Interpretive Center)

By September, 1885, the donations had been so generous that it accounted for over half of Whitman's income for the year. With some of the funds, his friends were able to buy Whitman a horse and buggy so that the frail poet would not be "house-tied." With tears in his eyes, Whitman happily boarded the phaeton and took a tour of the entire city of Camden.

Despite his limited mobility, Whitman continued to work and entertain an array of international guests at his humble home in Camden, that he was fond of calling his "shanty" or "coop." The young Bram Stoker, of future *Dracula* fame, had written effusive letters of praise to Whitman in the late 1870's and visited him three times at his home. The twenty-eight year old Irish poet and playwright, Oscar Wilde, a Whitman devotee since childhood, spent time at Mickle Street during the latter part of 1881. Whitman bonded immediately with these men and was flattered by "the attention of these two splendid boys." Wilde later sent a large photograph of himself to "the grand old man" with a note that says "there is no one in this great wide world of America whom I love and honor so much." (Whitman Interpretive Center)

When Whitman was not entertaining at Mickle Street or visiting friends around the city, he traveled along the eastern seaboard to give his famed Lincoln Lecture. Whitman's fascination with and admiration for Abraham Lincoln dates back to pre-Civil War days when Whitman identified with the politician's view for America as well as his moral and philosophical ideals. Following his assassination in 1865, Whitman composed a poetic tribute to the fallen leader, called "When Lilacs Last in the Dooryard Bloom'd," which, according to author Reynolds, was "a free-flowing poem in which three images—the western star (Lincoln), the singing thrush (the poet), and the lilac (his poem offered in eulogy),—interweave with meditations on death and the war."

In early 1879, Whitman was invited to give a talk on Lincoln at Steck Hall in Manhattan before a group of almost 100 people. The event went so well that Whitman's reputation as a public speaker became known, and for the next eleven years, he traveled between New York, Baltimore, Boston, Camden and Philadelphia giving what had become known as "The Lincoln Lecture," each time ending with a recitation of his well-known poem, "O Captain! My Captain!" Whitman would often stay with wealthy patrons who bathed him with gifts, carriage rides and lavish suites while traveling. Lecturing, he soon discovered, had many fringe benefits and it paid fairly well, too—his most profitable tour was in April, 1887 at Madison Square Theatre when he grossed over $600 for an evening's work.

"O Captain! My Captain" was one of the few Whitman poems that would become popular during his lifetime. It is only one of two poems in *Leaves of Grass* that rhyme and that appealed to the reading public; however, Whitman himself found its' rhyme and meter too conventional, remarking "I'm almost sorry I ever wrote the poem." (Swerdlow, 139)

It reads:

> O Captain! my Captain! our fearful trip is done,
> The ship has weather'd every rack, the prize we sought is won,
> The port is near, the bells I hear, the people all exulting
> While follow eyes the steady keel, the vessel grim and daring;
> But O heart! heart! heart!
> O the bleeding drops of red,
> Where on the deck my Captain lies,
> Fallen cold and dead.

The following year, 1888, Whitman suffered his second stroke—this one much more serious—left the aging poet severely paralyzed. Despite this, however, he managed in 1889, the year of his 70th birthday, to publish the eighth edition of *Leaves of Grass* with the assistance of his beloved friend, Horace Traubel. With the release of this pocket size volume, Whitman had finally made it into the "hip pocket" of his readers. This edition included a Prefatory Letter to the readers in which Whitman addresses the reader saying that "today finishes my 70th year; and ... I suppose I must reel out something to celebrate my old birthday anniversary, and for this special edition of the latest completest L. of G. utterance." Also included was an essay entitled "A Backward Glance O'er Travel'd Roads" and an annex of 65 new poems entitled "Sands at Seventy."

Primarily the reminisces of the elderly, housebound poet, these poems evoked memories for Whitman of a life fully lived, from his childhood days along the Long Island seashore, to his war experience, Broadway days and poetic mission. Finally, however, Whitman, always the commoner, celebrates the ordinary events of an extraordinary life and expresses gratitude to all who have traveled across the landscape of his life.

In "Thanks in Old Age" the wise poet writes:

Thanks in old age—thanks ere I go,
For health, the midday sun, the impalpable air—for life, mere life,
 For precious ever-lingering memories, (of you my mother dear-you
      Father—you, brothers, sisters, friends,)
For all my days—not those of peace along—the days of war the
      same,
For gentle words, caresses, gifts from foreign lands,
For shelter, wine and meat—for sweet appreciation,
(You distant, dim unknown—or young or old—countless, unspecified,
      readers belov'd,
We never met, and ne'er shall meet-and yet our souls embrace,
      long, close and long;)
For beings, groups, love, deeds, words, books—for colors, forms,
... Thanks—joyful thanks!—a soldier's, traveler's thanks.

His health delicate and suffering great physical pain daily, Whitman however, continued to press himself, compiling yet another edition in 1891, which included his farewell poems entitled "Good-Bye My Fancy." A slim edition of 32 new poems, these were the final verses Whitman was to write and his awareness of impending death is evident in the titles: "To the Sun-Set Breeze," "Old Chants," "Sail Out for Good, Eidolon Yacht!," "Sounds of the Winter," and "A Twilight Song."

Whitman, determined to combine his works into one volume, worked on a final comprehensive edition which included "Good-Bye My Fancy" as a concluding annex. In early December, 1891, Whitman sent an advance copy of this final edition of *Leaves of Grass* to his friend, Maurice Bucke. Excitedly, Whitman wrote, *"Leaves of Grass at last complete*—after 33 y'rs of hackling at it, all times & moods of my life, fair weather & foul, all parts of the land, and peace & war, young & old—."

This "deathbed edition," as it has become known, was published shortly before Whitman's death in March, 1892. These writings reflect a peaceful and calm poet, ready to meet his next challenge, confident that the solidarity of spirit he experienced in this life will accompany him to the next life:

Long have we lived, joy'd, caress'd together;
Delightful!—now separation—Good-bye my Fancy
Yet let me not be too hasty,
Long indeed have we lived, slept, filter'd, become really blended
   into one;
Then if we die we die together, (yes, we'll remain one,)
If we go anywhere we'll go together to meet what happens,
May-be we'll be better off and blither, and learn something,
May-be it is yourself now really ushering me to the true songs,
   (who knows?)
May-be it is you the mortal knob really undoing, turning—so
   now finally,
Good-bye—and hail! my Fancy.

On a rainy Saturday afternoon, March 26, 1892, Walt Whitman died at his home on Mickle Street in Camden, New Jersey following a lengthy illness resulting from a series of debilitating strokes. He was 72 years old.

In 1889 in the eighth edition of *Leaves of Grass*, an aging Whitman wrote that "I have not gained the acceptance of my own time from a worldly and business point of view. *Leaves of Grass* has been worse than a failure. The only comfort of the whole business is that I have had my say entirely my own way and put it unerringly on record."

Despite the fact that Whitman the *author* was not fully absorbed by the American public, Walt the *person*—from the little lad running on Long Island beaches, to the New York City dandy, to the Civil War wound dresser, to the gentle, aging poet—was embraced, admired and loved by thousands of his countrymen—longshoremen and luminaries alike. The outpouring of emotion and the celebration of his soul during the days between his death and funeral would have gladdened and warmed his heart.

Thousands of people filed into Whitman's humble home in Camden, paying final respects to the fallen poet who lay in a simple oak casket, covered with flowers sent from admirers the world over. It was a mixed crowd—fellow poets as well as family, friends (including Peter Doyle) and commonfolk.

John Burroughs, Whitman's longtime friend and author of the first biography of Whitman in 1863, wrote of the funeral, "When I saw the crowds of common people that flocked to Walt Whitman's funeral, I said, How fit, how touching, all this is how well it would please him. It is from the common people, the great army of workers, that he rises and speaks with such authority." (Reynolds, 588-89).

Whitman was buried in Harleigh Cemetery in Haddonfield, New Jersey in a massive, yet plain, granite mausoleum he had commissioned before his death.

Walt Whitman remained true to his poetic mission to the end of his life. He worked tirelessly to gain an audience for his lifelong work, *Leaves of Grass*, but in the end had only minor success—his poetry was never as "fully absorbed" by Americans as he had hoped during his lifetime. He predicted, however, that his "audience would lay in the future" and once again the wise poet was right. In *Leaves of Grass*, Whitman created a portrait of himself and his times that continues to excite, inspire and touch readers the world over.

A plaque at the Interpretive Center at The Walt Whitman Birthplace sums up Whitman and his remarkable life best:

> Whitman's lasting influence in America is inestimable. He single-handedly liberated American verse from the shadow of European literature by cultivating a voice that unmistakably sang AMERICA!!! By carrying poetry out of the parlor and into the streets, he challenged all Americans to participate in his profoundly egalitarian view of the world. Whitman's courage in speaking out about issues often suppressed injustices ... he continues to provoke and inspire us. Whitman holds his place among us as one of the most loving humanists that this country has produced.

Works Cited

Baym, Nina, et. al. *The Norton Anthology of American Literature II.* 3rd edition, New York: W.W. Norton, 1989.

Baym, Nina, et. al. *The Norton Anthology of American Literature.* Shorter 4th edition, New York: W.W. Norton, 1995.

Bloom, Harold, *Walt Whitman.* (Bloom's Major Poets). Philadelphia: Chelsea House Publishers, 1999.

Leipold, L. Edmond, *Famous American Poets.* Minneapolis: T.S. Denison & Co., 1969.

Polley, Robert, ed. *America the Beautiful in the Words of Walt Whitman.* Waukesha, Wisconsin: Country Beautiful Corp., 1970.

Reynolds, David S., *Walt Whitman's America: A Cultural Biography.* New York: Knopf, 1995.

Swerdlow, Joel L., "America's Poet: Walt Whitman," *National Geographic,* December 1994, pp. 106-141.

Whitman, Walt, *The Portable Walt Whitman,* Mark Van Doren, ed., New York: Viking Press, 1977.

Whitman, Walt, *Leaves of Grass,* Harold W. Blodgett and E. Sculley Bradley, editors. New York: W.W. Norton and Co., 1985.

Zweig, Paul, "The Wound Dresser" in *Modern Critical Views,* Harold Bloom, ed. Philadelphia: Chelsea House Publishers, 1985. pp. 143-157.

MATT LONGABUCCO

"The Proof of a Poet"—Walt Whitman and His Critics

Is Walt Whitman who he says he is? That is, is he a native and naive genius, a plainspeaker who broke radically with poetic tradition, a conduit for the voice of his age, and a human divinity whose bushy white beard signifies an all-fatherhood to the people and poets who follow him? Perhaps more interesting than the question itself is the resistance which the Whitman persona has offered to the efforts of postmodern skeptics and enthusiastic biographers alike. Whitman turns out to be an emotional topic, so bound up is the poet—as he always sought to be— with the consciousness of his nation. It would be hard to think of a writer who more profoundly embodies the dreams, myths, and anxieties that America has for itself.

Whitman's mature poetic career began around 1850, when he started writing the twelve poems that were to become his book *Leaves of Grass*. He published the first edition in 1855, paying the printing costs and even setting some of the type (he had been a printer). Many have come to view this first edition as so significant as to eclipse all others, and seen the remainder of Whitman's career as one long denouement punctuated at times by brilliant aftershocks. Certainly it was an achievement that seemed, especially at the time, to come from out of nowhere, though Whitman had been a writer beforehand and undeniable influences for his thought exist.

The frontispiece of the 1855 *Leaves of Grass* features an engraved portrait of Whitman, based on a daguerreotype, in lieu of the author's name on the title page. The young bearded man is depicted in a casual posture, one hand in his pocket and the other on his hip, sporting workman's clothes, and looking directly at the viewer with an expression blank enough to be read as anything from arrogance to abstractedness. Much has been made of this design choice of Whitman's, since it seems to announce two important thematic premises of the book: first, that the poet is not separable from his physical body (and therefore his portrait is as valid an identification as his name), and second, that the poet is "one of the roughs," as he puts it, "no stander above men and women or apart from them" (and therefore dressed like the mass of working men and women). Whitman elsewhere states that in giving the public his book he is giving them himself, his actual person; the public that receives this gift is not the intellectual public but the larger public, in fact the republic or the people who make up the American democracy.

Whitman articulates the necessity for such a transaction in the untitled preface to *Leaves of Grass*. He begins, as any good rhetorician might, with the concession that "America does not repel the past," but the reader quickly comes to feel that for Whitman there is little of "the corpse" of tradition in "the stalwart and wellshaped heir who approaches." This is the first of many instances in which Whitman figures history as teleological and America as its inevitable outcome: "The United States themselves are essentially the greatest poem," he writes. The present moment, however, is all potentiality, a set of optimum conditions:

> Here are the roughs and beards and space and ruggedness and nonchalance that the soul loves. Here the performance disdaining the trivial unapproached in the tremendous audacity of its crowds and groupings and the push of its perspective spreads with crampless and flowing breadth and showers its prolific and splendid extravagance. One sees it must indeed own the riches of the summer and winter, and need never be bankrupt while corn grows from the ground or the orchards drop apples or the bays contain fish or men beget children upon women. (Whitman 5)

The short passage describes many of the crucial elements of the promising nation: the working people, among whom Whitman belongs (he, too, is a "rough" whose nonchalance the reader has just seen in his pose on the frontispiece), a largeness of purpose, a sense of abundance—even a mandate to be abundant—in both cities and in nature, and a procreative sexuality attuned to the richness and largeness of the land. Whitman conveys urgency in his prose; faced with the arrival of such fecundity, there is little time to stop and breathe over commas.

Still, the nation's promise "awaits the gigantic and generous treatment worthy of it;" it provides the raw material but requires the intervention of a figure to give it voice (Whitman 6). This figure—the poet—is a complicated and sometimes contradictory one for Whitman, being both of and from the people, but also unique among them, prophetic as to the vast scope of the possibilities they contain, and necessary to the achievement of such prophecies. He is both unspecial and unique: "he is complete in himself.... the others are as good as he, only he sees it and they do not" (Whitman 10).

Moreover, Whitman specifies the actual terms of the society that the poet will prepare the people to create. Thus, because the poet "sees eternity in men and women ... he does not see men and women as dreams or dots," the outcome shall be that "no man thenceforward shall be degraded for ignorance or weakness or sin" (Whitman 9-10). The poet shows the way to an acceptance and exaltation of men and women and all common things. Whitman (for he is, after all, the poet in question) even takes on the formulations of the sermon; he preaches:

> This is what you shall do: Love the earth and sun and the animals, despise riches, give alms to every one that asks, stand up for the stupid and crazy, devote your income and labor to others, hate tyrants, argue not concerning God, have patience and indulgence toward the people, take off your hat to nothing known or unknown or to any man or number of men, go freely with powerful uneducated persons and with the young and with the mothers of families, read these leaves in the open air every season of every year of your life, re-examine all you have been told at school or church or in any book, dismiss whatever insults your own soul ... (Whitman 11)

These are nothing less than the instructions for a perfect, spiritual democracy, with a touch of good humor in the effort (the injunction to read Whitman's book every day is followed by the caveat to re-examine the contents of all books). More importantly, Whitman implies that the method for achieving such a society is to improve the individuals—for it is to individual readers that these commandments are addressed—who make up this society. This is democracy that goes one member at a time, or to make a pun on something that is more than a pun, the grassroots approach of *Leaves of Grass*.

There is more at stake for Whitman, however, than politics and place; if America is an ideal jumping-off point, it is not only that for its own sake, but because it empowers the poet to achieve an otherwise unrealizable transcendence. As Whitman's great biographer, Gay Wilson Allen, puts it: "What Walt Whitman wanted most in his life of the imagination was to immerse, to bathe, to float ... in the eternal stream of existence" (Allen 144). If that makes Whitman sound like a detached mystic, no less did he recognize the life of the body and the potential to wallow in evil; he writes of "venereal sores or discolorations," "the putrid veins of gluttons or rumdrinkers," "serpentine poison of those that seduce women," "attainment of gains by discreditable means," and "harshness of officers to men or judges to prisoners or fathers to sons or sons to fathers or of husbands to wives or bosses to their boys" (Whitman 21). Nor is he unaware of the vulgar materialism his countrymen often display.

Whitman had once written in the margin of a review he was reading: "The perfect poem is simple, healthy, natural—no griffins, angels, centaurs—no hysterics or blue fire—no dyspepsia, no suicidal intentions" (Allen 132). This jotted memorandum manages to express Whitman's preference for natural, spoken-sounding (though rhythmic) poetic language; for subject matter drawn from everyday life instead of mythology or legend; for an unpretentious, if sometimes elevated, voice and diction; and for a poetics of exaltation rather than a performance of melancholy. In the preface, Whitman sketches out a poetic program for himself that calls for a lack of ornament and the appearance of effortlessness in his verse; he is not blind to the rhetorical dimension of any text but feels that the poet must proceed "without exposing in the least how it is done ..." (Whitman 12). Yet Whitman just as often writes as if rhetoric could be entirely superseded: "What I tell I tell for precisely what it is ... What I experience or portray shall go from my composition without a shred of my composition. You shall stand by my side and look in the mirror with me" (Whitman 14). How can the poet who is aware of not "exposing" his methods (therefore admitting that he has methods) still proclaim that the "composition" of his body and soul can be conveyed without rhetorical "composition"? If there is an answer, it lies in Whitman's desire to be like Nature, which he views as guileless in its practical simplicity but which still contains deeper workings and secret logic. For Whitman, the poet is to Nature as the reader is to the poet: Nature or the poet presents itself to be beheld, and stands beside you in the mirror, but the quality of the poet or the reader's looking is always a matter of partial seeing or seeing with difficulty, and the object in the mirror is looking at you as much and as closely as you yourself are looking at it.

The preface, with its prose broken by ellipses, its long catalogs, and its imaginative movement across large periods of history and wide expanses of geography, formally prefigures the poems that are to follow. The poems are in free verse in long unrhymed lines often described as prose-like, and given to direct address to the reader, prophetic language, and lists of images, names, and evaluations.

The first, long, untitled poem in the 1855 edition is one of Whitman's best-known. In later editions it would be called "Song of Myself" and divided into sections, but in this first incarnation it merely announced itself as the deed which had arrived to enact the preface's word. Here is its famous beginning:

> I celebrate myself,
> And what I assume you shall assume,
> For every atom belonging to me as good belongs to you.
>
> I loafe and invite my soul,
> I lean and loafe at my ease .... observing a spear of summer grass.
> (Whitman 27)

The sense of expansiveness in this poem—what Whitman would call the "dilation" of the self—caused some later critics to argue that its genesis had been a moment of intensely heightened consciousness such as religious mystics claim to experience. Even if that were the case, the experience has been fed and expanded in light of Whitman's philosophical tenets and poetic project. He has little use for any dogma regarding a fallen world; rather all things seem to him totally sufficient:

> There was never any more inception than there is now,
> Nor any more youth or age than there is now;
> And will never be any more perfection than there is now,
> Nor any more heaven or hell than there is now.
>
> (Whitman 28)

And he cannot react but with pleasure: "The delight alone or in the rush of the streets, or along the fields and hillsides,/The feeling of health .... the full-noon trill .... the song of me rising from bed and meeting the sun;" and "I dote on myself .... there is that lot of me, and all so luscious,/Each moment and whatever happens thrills me with joy" (Whitman 27, 55).

　　Is Whitman then indiscriminate, unable to choose what is fit to be in his poem, and an egotist besides? To the last charge he replies, "I know perfectly well my own egotism," but this is a gag; Whitman would not be the true Romantic that he is if he did not see his inner self as continuous with, or reflective of, nature and the outside world. To dote on himself is to dote on all of creation. And far from being indiscriminate, the poem's inclusiveness—which is after all the approach by which it seeks to distinguish itself as a new literature—is balanced by the specificity and keenness of the images and feelings he records. Further, Whitman enables himself to import, with the rest, aspects of the world that might (in fact they did) offend his readers' sensibilities in terms of modernity, sexuality, class, ethnicity, and race. A small part of one of the longer catalogs illustrates the gamut:

> The conductor beats time for the band and all the performers follow him,
> The child is baptised—the convert is making the first professions,
> The regatta is spread on the bay .... how the white sails sparkle!
> The drover watches his drove, he sings out to them that would stray,
> The pedlar sweats with his pack on his back—the purchaser higgles about the odd
> 　　　cent,
> The camera and plate are prepared, the lady must sit for her daguerrotype,
> The bride unrumples her white dress, the minutehand of the clock moves
> slowly,
> The opium eater reclines with rigid head and just-opened lips,
> The prostitute draggles her shawl, her bonnet bobs on her tipsy and pimpled
> 　　　neck ...
>
> (Whitman 41)

Included as well are the President, deckhands, a "connoisseur," a slave being auctioned, and a Native American squaw, among many others. One gets the sense that a notebook full of impressions has been sacrificed for a page of verse. Of course none of these catalogs is in any sense complete, though they are ambitiously large; Whitman, who has little use for metaphor and simile (ornaments, he might say), proceeds instead by metonymy and synecdoche, so that some objects, images, and people are made to stand in for everything that exists. Whitman, in striving to be democratic, employs the very technique by which America is democratic—the representation, by some things, of all things.

We have seen how concerned Whitman is with manifesting an actual person in his lines. He names the subjective consciousness that is inherent in, and conveyed by, his work "Personality," with parts "physical, emotional, moral, intellectual, and aesthetic." In one poem he declares, "I and mine do not convince by arguments, similes, rhymes,/We convince by our presence." In another poem he insists, "The words of my book nothing, the drift of it everything;" this "drift" is the presence of Personality that informs the text. In "Song of Myself" he calls himself "Walt Whitman, an American, one of the roughs, a kosmos...," and later he brags: "I am large.... I contain multitudes." He takes on all citizenships, becoming "A southerner soon as a northerner," and he travels "by experience" through the nineteenth-century United States, into the depths of depravity, and across time and space:

Voyaging to every port to dicker and adventure;
Hurrying with the modern crowd, as eager and fickle as any,
Hot toward one I hate, ready in my madness to knife him;
Solitary at midnight in my back yard, my thoughts gone from me a long while,
Walking the old hills of Judea with the beautiful gentle god by my side;
Speeding through space .... speeding through heaven and the stars,
Speeding amid the seven satellites and the broad ring and the diameter of eighty
    thousand miles,
Speeding with tailed meteors .... throwing fire-balls like the rest ...
                                        (Whitman 62-3)

There are as many moods here as locations, and it is intensity of feeling that grounds the fantasy in truth.

The Personality's still greater variety comes out in relation to others. Whitman echoes the preface in ascribing himself a poet's greater ability to see compared to others when he says that people are "all just as immortal and fathomless as myself;/They do not know how immortal, but I know" (Whitman 33). But then: "These are the thoughts of all men in all ages and lands, they are not original with me,/If they are not yours as much as mine they are nothing or next to nothing" (Whitman 43). And sometimes he grows intimate: "This hour I tell things in confidence,/I might not tell everybody but I will tell you" (Whitman 45). His compassion is boundless—"I see myself in prison shaped like another man,/And feel the dull intermitted pain"—as is his generosity: "... any thing I have I bestow" (Whitman 70, 72). He offers comfort, as well, telling any "despairer," "Hang your whole weight upon me" (Whitman 73). He is so sensual as to feel all others' presence ecstatically: "To touch my person to some one else's is about as much as I can stand" (Whitman 55). And then he is lonesome and apart from any other, as in the "twenty-ninth bather" section, in which the poet watches a woman watching some men bathe nude in the river—we feel the speaker knows only too well her distance and longing. He is by turns brash, solipsistic, tender, delusional, pathetic, and kind.

It is tempting to read "Song of Myself" for autobiography, and many have. But even the speaker of the poem would complicate any simple notions we might have of the factual information we find within. Indeed, when "trippers and askers" interrogate him about his early life, his city and nation, news, his thoughts on literature, his love affairs, his moods, his health, and other subjects, Whitman seems to dismiss it all as so much gossip:

> They come to me days and nights and go from me again,
> But they are not the Me myself.
>
> Apart from the pulling and hauling stands what I am,
> Stands amused, complacent, compassionating, idle, unitary,
> Looks down, is erect, bends an arm on an impalpable certain rest,
> Looks with its sidecurved head curious what will come next,
> Both in and out of the game, and watching and wondering at it.
>   (Whitman 30)

This self is deeply split and not defined by circumstance. Nevertheless, readers have speculated, especially about questions of Whitman's views on slavery and his sexuality. As to the former, there is a passage in the poem in which he speaks of harboring a runaway slave—this is clearly not biographically true, but points to Whitman's sympathies—and yet he is often content to put black slaves in their appointed place along with all the other types and characters to whom he assigns a part in the new nation. Actually, Whitman's lifelong writings show that his position fluctuated in regard to slavery, although ultimately his opinion was probably close to that of Lincoln's in that he was mostly concerned with the issue in terms of the threat it posed to his beloved union.

As we shall see, many people have written about Whitman's almost certain homosexuality—a problematic notion, however, since in Whitman's time this category (and even the word "homosexual") did not exist as we know it today. Almost every discussion of this issue cites the following passage from "Song of Myself":

> I mind how we lay in June, such a transparent summer morning;
> You settled your head athwart my hips and gently turned over upon me,
> And parted the shirt from my bosom-bone, and plunged your tongue to my
>   barestript heart,
> And reached till you felt my beard, and reached till you held my feet.
>   (Whitman 30)

As it would not always be in later poems, the gender of the "you" is left unsaid here, and the nature of what is occurring has proven "obvious" to widely different interpretations. In his time, Whitman faced far more censure for his acceptance of figures like the prostitute, his sometimes frank sexual images (i.e. "a spirt of my own seminal wet"), and his insistence on the place of real sexuality in his universe: "Copulation is no more rank to me than death is," said the poet for whom "to die is different from what anyone supposed, and luckier" (Whitman 51, 73, 32). For Whitman, sexual liberation was part of the process by which individuals become better prepared to participate in democracy and even the grand cycles of the world or universe. As we shall see, critics have argued about the status of homosexuality as a vehicle toward such liberation.

"Song of Myself" is an optimistic leap into the infinite, a tract extolling the purest democracy, a plea for the fellowship of bodies, an embrace of life as well as death, and a summons to a population of promising minds. Always Whitman wants to assure us that he is providing no more than the heuristic by which we shall experience his dilation for ourselves, but then he is almost comic in his inability to leave us to it:

> I teach straying from me, yet who can stray from me?
> I follow you wherever you are from the present hour,
> My words itch at your ear till you understand them.
> I do not say these things for a dollar, or to fill up the time while I wait for a boat;
> It is you talking just as much as myself .... I act as the tongue of you,
> It was tied in your mouth .... in time it begins to be loosened.
>   (Whitman 83-4)

Whitman is addicted to the sense of being always with us. Near the end of the poem, he suggests "If you want me again look for me under your bootsoles;" as his *Leaves* stay with us, so too will his actual body return to the soil which Americans still tread (Whitman 88).

The remainder of the 1855 *Leaves of Grass* contains shorter lyrics which tend to recapitulate the ideas and techniques of the preface and the first poem. Among them are the poems that would become known as "I Sing the Body Electric" and "There Was a Child Went Forth." Whitman published the book in obscurity, and it probably only sold a handful of copies. Other copies were given away, and by a miraculous stroke of luck one particular recipient—Ralph Waldo Emerson—opened his copy and read it with satisfaction.

Thus it was that almost as soon as Whitman had a book he had the most eminent man of letters in the country for a critic. Emerson wrote Whitman a letter full of praise: "I greet you at the beginning of a great career, which yet must have had some foreground somewhere, for such a start. I rubbed my eyes a little, to see if this sunbeam were no illusion; but the solid sense of the book is a sober certainty. It has the best merits, namely, of fortifying and encouraging" (Whitman 1350). The great essayist was right in seeing that there was a "foreground" to *Leaves of Grass*, despite Whitman's apparent dismissal of the past.

Perhaps Emerson was attuned to Whitman's influences because his own work was chief among them. Whitman acknowledged this debt later when he said that he had been "simmering" until Emerson "brought him to a boil." He avowed that he had not read Emerson's essay "The Poet" until 1857, but this claim has been roundly rejected based on the undeniable presence of Emerson's concepts in the first *Leaves of Grass*. Of the relation of poet to people, for example, Emerson says:

> The breadth of the problem is great, for the poet is representative. He stands among partial men for the complete man, and apprises us not of wealth, but of the commonwealth. The young man reveres men of genius, because, to speak truly, they are more himself than he is. They receive of the soul as he also receives, but they more. (Emerson 218)

Again and again in *Leaves of Grass* we see this formulation of the poet as the man who represents all men but whose vision is superior to them and necessary for their development. "The Poet" calls for an American poetry to deal with American subjects; it suggests that "bare lists of words" may in themselves be poetic; it suggests that the poet voyage the earth in his imagination. And Emerson constructs a prototype of Whitman's Personality, writing: "All form is an effect of character; all condition, of the quality of the life; all harmony, of health ..." (Emerson 222).

Whitman was more widely read than he sometimes pretended to be. *Leaves of Grass* results in many respects from his understanding of Homer, Lucretius, Dante, the Old and New Testament, Shakespeare, the novels of George Sand, Heine and Goethe, Voltaire and Hugo, Walter Scott and Tennyson, and Carlyle. He knew the English Romantic poets and the German idealists Kant, Fichte, Schelling, and Hegel. He said that he had read some "Hindoo" texts, and scholars like V.K. Chari have identified the presence of Eastern thought in Whitman's poetry. He was particularly affected by Frances Wright's *A Few Days in Athens*—which espoused a kind of neo-Epicureanism—and the revolutionary philosophy he found in the Count de Volney's *Ruins* and the works of Thomas Paine. Literary theory came to him from contemporary English periodicals. Whitman picked up the latest thinking in such diverse fields as astronomy, Egyptology, and phrenology (the bogus science that purported to ascertain personality types by measuring the human skull). In his New York milieu he was stimulated by the theater (which he adored) and especially his lifelong love of Italian opera. And he was an eyewitness to the surging growth of both the city and the nation, whose trials and triumphs constituted their own influential text.

Whitman had also been a prolific, if undistinguished, writer before 1855. In his capacity as a newspaper editor he had penned editorials, essays, and political broadsides; written and published conventional poems and short stories; and even written a didactic temperance novel entitled *Franklin Evans, or the Inebriate* (1842). Moreover, he spent some time in the company of members of the so-called "Young America" movement, and though he later downplayed his connection to them, it is clear that he was inspired by their ambition to establish an American literature that would repudiate the English tradition and work actively to achieve democratic ideals. Allen quotes this description of Young American doctrine: "They shifted the approach to poetry from the text of the poem to the 'maker' or 'creator' of the poem"—clearly a resonant idea for Whitman (Allen 129).

Whitman published a second edition of *Leaves of Grass* in 1860. It included 33 poems (among them versions of "Song of the Open Road" and "Salut au Monde!"); the preface was gone; and Whitman reprinted Emerson's letter in the back (without consulting Emerson). Whitman's prose contribution was an open "response" to Emerson, in which he addressed Emerson as "Master" and rearticulated his poetic program. In the same year Whitman wrote a political tract entitled "The Eighteenth Presidency!" which lodged an emotional plea against the divisive actions of Southern slaveowners.

The second edition contained one of Whitman's lyric master-pieces, called "Sun-Down Poem" at first but better-known by its later title, "Crossing Brooklyn Ferry." The poet is riding an East River ferry, and is overwhelmed by a sense of sympathy with future generations:

Others will see the islands large and small;
Fifty years hence, others will see them as they cross, the sun half an hour high,
A hundred years hence, or ever so many hundred years hence, others will see
    them,
Will enjoy the sunset, the pouring-in of the flood tide, the falling-back to the sea
    of the ebb-tide.

It avails not, time nor place—distance avails not,
I am with you, you men and women of a generation, or ever so many generations
    hence,
Just as you feel when you look on the river and sky, so I felt ...
                     (Whitman 308-9)
                     (All remaining quotations are from the
                     final edition of *Leaves of Grass*.)

Even those who read this address across time as a pure rhetorical device must feel a sense of uncanniness reading these lines. Many thoughts and feelings are being expressed in this passage—eternal vision, sadness over the poet's own inevitable death, jealousy of the future, a great message through time of enduring humanity—but they all coexist in a kind of richness that often remains mired in mere contradiction in "Song of Myself." In this poem, too, we can see already the curious nature of all of Whitman's work after what he called the "barbaric yawp" of the 1855 *Leaves*. Almost from the start of his career he would be faced with the sense of having already produced a legacy, and we often find him asking questions of posterity; in "Crossing Brooklyn Ferry" he wonders, "My great thoughts as I supposed them, were they not in reality meagre?" (Whitman 311). The reader soon comes to realize that Whitman's personality was as much an ideal for him as it seems to us.

    Whitman was perfecting his voice by this time, using repetition, echo, chiasmus, parallelism, and reiteration to make his long unrhymed lines rhythmic. He retained his gift for imagery, as when in "Crossing Brooklyn Ferry" he "Look'd at the fine centrifugal spokes of light round the shape of my head in the sunlit water" (Whitman 310). The 1860 *Leaves of Grass* included still more fine poems, including "Starting from Paumanok," "As I Ebb'd with the Ocean of Life," and "Out of the Cradle Endlessly Rocking." The third edition was the first to group the poems into sections: "Chants Democratic," "Leaves of Grass," "Enfans d'Adam," and "Live-Oak Leaves." The latter two would eventually become the "Children of Adam" poems, which dealt with sexuality and which Emerson and many others advised Whitman to expurgate (he never did), and the "Calamus" poems, which treated male friendship and—though not explicitly for Whitman's original readers— homosexuality (or at least homoeroticism) as well. "I Saw in Louisiana a Live-Oak Growing" is one of the best-known poems from the "Calamus" section. In it, Whitman identifies with a solitary live oak that "utters joyous leaves of dark green," but ultimately resists the identification because he cannot remain as solitary as the tree:

> Yet it remains to me a curious token, it makes me think of manly love;
> For all that, and though the live-oak glistens there in Louisiana solitary in a wide
> > flat space,
> Uttering joyous leaves all its life without a friend a lover near,
> I know very well I could not.
>
> (Whitman 280)

During the Civil War, Whitman volunteered in hospitals at the front and in Washington, D.C., tending to wounded soldiers and watching with apprehension as his beloved nation attempted to secure its own survival. In 1865, he published *Drum-Taps* and *Sequel to Drum-Taps*. The former contained many poems dealing with the war, including "Beat! Beat! Drums!" "Cavalry Crossing a Ford," and "By the Bivouac's Fitful Flame." The sequel contained the famous elegies written in the wake of Lincoln's assassination, "When Lilacs Last in the Dooryard Bloom'd" and the endlessly anthologized (and uncharacteristic) "O Captain! My Captain!"

Whitman's prose contributions include a three-part prose work entitled *Democratic Vistas* (1870), in which he takes up the question of how to properly form a true democratic society. He also wrote *Specimen Days* (1882), a collection of sketches that includes memoirs of his youth and influences, of nineteenth-century New York, and of the war. Some of the sketches reveal much about their author's mind; how could Whitman not love naming things, for example, when he tells us in "Omnibus Jaunts and Drivers" that he knew bus drivers called "Broadway Jack, Dressmaker, Balky Bill, George Storms, Old Elephant, his brother Young Elephant ..., Tippy, Pop Rice, Big Frank, Yellow Joe,

Pete Callahan, Patsy Dee, and dozens more ..." (Whitman 727). He records his impressions of the soldiers' hospitals, and includes travel-sketches like "The Women of the West." Rare literary observations appear in pieces such as "Edgar Poe's Significance" and "My Tribute to Four Poets" (they are Emerson, Longfellow, Bryant, and Whittier). Idyllic pieces like "The First Frost-Mems" are lovely prose-poems recalling Whitman's happy seasons at Timber Creek.

For the rest of his career, Whitman would bring out small books of poems or combinations of poetry and prose—*Passage to India* (1870), *Two Rivulets* (1876), *November Boughs* (1888), *Good-Bye my Fancy* (1891)—and eventually incorporate the poetry into the ever-multiplying sections and annexes of *Leaves of Grass*. The titles of poems and their groupings changed with each edition. There was a fourth edition in 1867, a fifth in 1870, and a "Centennial" edition in 1876. The 1881 edition ends with the poem "So Long!" in which Whitman is still pursuing his goal of living fully on the page, speaking intimately with the reader:

> Camerado, this is no book,
> Who touches this touches a man,
> (Is it night? are we here together alone?)
> It is I you hold and who holds you,
> I spring from the pages into your arms—decease calls me forth.
>
> (Whitman 611)

The final, or "Deathbed," edition (1891-92) contains 383 poems. Whitman had put out a *Complete Poems and Prose* in 1888, but for the final *Leaves* he appended a note decreeing, "As there are now several editions of L. of G., different texts and dates, I wish to say that I prefer and recommend this present one, complete, for future printing, if there should be any ..." (Whitman 148).

Why did Whitman begin and end with *Leaves of Grass*, the book he was to call "that unkillable work!"? In purely practical terms, Whitman was a shrewd marketer who knew that the title of his book had gained fame and infamy. To be sure, his revisions were not always for the best, and as he fiddled with 25-year-old poems he sometimes inadvertently defanged them, or regularized their punctuation and diction in such a way as to make the 1855 edition appear all the more raw and, paradoxically, more unified. His biographer Allen points to Whitman's seeming obliviousness to what was good and worth keeping as opposed to what to jettison and forget. But these arguments are beside the point; for Whitman, *Leaves of Grass* was not just a "collected poems," but his very Person. The leaves—the poems—make a field, the earth from which the poet comes and to which he will return in death; and this earth is at the same time the soil of the nation that nourished his genius. Other metaphors Whitman applied to his work in progress include a tree with rings of age, a city, and a cathedral. And his choice to revise rather than replace reflected the state of the republic—for Whitman was not insensible to the supreme act of revision he had witnessed in the Civil War and Reconstruction. Democracy too is an ongoing text.

At the close of the preface to the 1855 edition, Whitman offers a critical acid-test by which he himself presumably expects to be judged: "The proof of a poet is that his country absorbs him as affectionately as he has absorbed it." Certainly many poets could live with absorption alone, but Whitman reveals much of his character in placing the burden of "proof" on the level of affection. He reminds us of a lover asking, with roundabout insistence, if he is loved in return as much as he loves. It is a fraught situation for a critic, who is being asked to judge the man along with the text. Whitman framed the challenge in another way in a late piece of prose: "No one will get at my verses who insists upon viewing them as a literary performance, or attempt at such performance, or as aiming mainly toward art or aestheticism" (Whitman 671). In a way, then, Whitman invited both the moralistic scorn and fanatical devotion that characterized the first hundred years of discourse about *Leaves of Grass*. He presented the public with a broad persona and they reacted to it broadly.

Charles A. Dana's review of the first *Leaves of Grass*, in the New York *Daily Tribune*, is exemplary in judging Whitman's persona on its own terms:

> [Whitman's *Leaves of Grass*] are certainly original in their external form, have been shaped on no pre-existent model out of the author's own brain. Indeed, his independence often becomes coarse and defiant. His language is too frequently reckless and indecent though this appears to arise from a naive unconsciousness rather than from an impure

mind. His words might have passed between Adam and Eve
in Paradise, before the want of fig-leaves brought no shame;
but they are quite out of place amid the decorum of modern
society ... (Dana 5)

Whitman could hardly complain about being dismissed by this reviewer
as an "odd genius," since he had courted the role of the "naive" and
unconscious natural man. But he probably did not see that the logic of
the "noble savage" or "child of nature"—a logic his persona seemed to
ratify—was at the same time being used to justify the oppression of
Native and African-Americans. Those people were also supposedly
"naive," and therefore "out of place amid the decorum of modern
society."

Charles Eliot Norton is more harsh in *Putnam's Monthly*, asserting
that Whitman has simply produced prose and parsed it "without any
idea or sense of reason." He calls the book's language "laughable," and
suggests that Whitman is probably a working-class man regurgitating
poorly-understood transcendentalism. Referring to the grand claims of
the first poem, he quips: "That he was one of the roughs was also
tolerably plain; but that he was a kosmos, is a piece of news we were
hardly prepared for" (Norton 18). The *Criterion*'s Rufus W. Griswold,
who thinks *Leaves* "a mass of stupid filth," ends his review with a cryptic
admonition about the "stern duty" that will have to be done in regards
to Whitman. To clarify, he appends the Latin phrase *Peccatum illud
horribile, inter Christianos non nominandum* ("That horrible sin not to be
named among Christians") (Griswold 27). He appears to be calling for
the public decrial of a homosexual.

Further editions of *Leaves* garnered their share of abuse; book and
author were growing notorious, and proved an easy target. The
Christian Examiner complains, "So, then, these rank *Leaves* have
sprouted afresh," and frames its response as "not a question of literary
opinion principally, but of the very essence of religion and morality"
(*Christian* 59). And while the *Daily Times* admits that the second edition
has a "singular electric attraction," still it finds that Whitman is unaware
of intellectual history and megalomaniacal regarding his own literary
greatness: "Who is this arrogant young man who proclaims himself the
Poet of the Time, and who roots like a pig among a rotten garbage of
licentious thoughts?" (*Daily* 60).

Whitman was not entirely beset by detractors, though there were enough of them to dismay him. Of the scant reviews for the original *Leaves*, some were promising, and there was always Emerson's letter. Edward Everett Hale, in his piece for the *North American Review*, makes the seemingly self-evident point that literature from Homer onward had been full of "indelicate" material, and that it might appear a bit provincial for Americans to repudiate their most promising poets based on their own squeamishness. Fanny Fern, writing in the *New York Ledger* in 1856, is of the same mind; she prefers the forthrightness of *Leaves* to far more offensive material that artfully disguises its corruption. Whitman's plainspeaking is potentially liberating for all, causing Fern to effuse, "Walt Whitman, the effeminate world needed thee!" (Fern 46). And later Moncure D. Conway in the *Dial* defends Whitman's prosody as "biblical," and his inclusion of "profanity" as a necessary evil accompanying any true representation of the world (Conway 106).

For years, the British were more amenable Whitman critics than their American counterparts, at least in part because they were willing to defer to Emerson's opinion. William Michael Rossetti, who brought out a selected edition of Whitman's poems in England, places the poet in the pantheon with Shakespeare. He convinced his friend Anne Gilchrist to publish her thoughts on Whitman; she certifies his verse as entirely rhythmic if not conventionally metrical, and admires his "electric streams" even if she is "obliged to lay the book down for a while" when emotion overcomes her (Gilchrist 83). Algernon Charles Swinburne's "To Walt Whitman in America" hails Whitman in verse; later, however, Swinburne regretted his enthusiasm and ran down the American in an 1887 issue of *The Fortnightly Review*.

No survey of the contemporary criticism would be complete without acknowledging one of Whitman's most prolific critics—himself. His newspaper connections allowed him to place numerous anonymous pieces meant to steer public opinion to a proper appreciation of his work. His favorite tactic in these reviews is to play the visionary critic who hails the long-awaited prophet: "An American bard at last! One of the roughs, large, proud, affectionate, eating, drinking, and breeding, his costume manly and free, his face sunburnt and bearded, his posture strong and erect, his voice bringing hope and prophecy to the generous races of young and old" (Whitman 8). He would have us accept, apparently, a criticism of the body to match his poetics of one. The ruse is made even more transparent by the recognizable prose, the call to nationhood, and the insistence that this poet is without previous influences. He predicts that the poet will write "the great psalm of the republic," and even speculates that the man would be ideal to hold public office as a sort of philosopher-king. Whitman shows off his isolationist side when reviewing *Leaves* alongside a new book from Tennyson. He wants a clean break from the English tradition; as he warns elsewhere, "Has not literature been bred in and in long enough?" (Whitman Review 13).

As Whitman's life and career drew to a close, many of his harsh critics faded away, and the grand old man was toasted by devotees and hagiographers. These are the so-called "hot little prophets," as Bliss Perry names them in his 1906 biography of Whitman; Swinburne labels them "Whitmaniacs." In fact, many of them made useful contributions to future scholarship, such as Horace Traubel, whose conversations with Whitman in the last years of the poet's life resulted in the six-volume *With Walt Whitman in Camden* (1906-1982). Whitman's friend William Douglas O'Connor wrote "The Good Gray Poet" (1866) to praise Whitman, but he also strikes a necessary blow against censorship. John Burroughs and Richard Bucke wrote similarly laudatory pieces.

Whitman fell somewhat out of critical favor in the early twentieth century; T.S. Eliot and the early New Critics, especially, were not very interested in him. As James E. Miller, Jr. was to describe the situation from the vantage point of 1979:

> The irrelevance of Whitman seemed permanently established when the academies and the little magazines all extolled the consciously structured, elaborately patterned, brilliantly imaged, rigorously impersonal, subtly ironic poem. All poetry was remeasured, and when it smacked of the naively celebratory, the expansively confessional, the intuitively shaped, the shamelessly personal, the improvisationally spoken or chanted, it was dismissed with amusement or contempt; the well-made poem rendered Whitman obsolete. (Miller 289)

A number of famous writers, however, were compelled to at least voice an opinion, perhaps aware that Whitman would one day be considered, with Emily Dickinson, the starting-point for modern American poetry. Thoreau had once found him "awfully good," with reservations; a young Henry James was cruel to *Drum-Taps*, as was William Dean Howells; Oscar Wilde, who visited Whitman during his American tour, wrote a piece full of admiration in 1889. Willa Cather considered him well-meaning but misguided in his choice to write of the ugly as well as the beautiful, while William James found him congenial to his own philosophy. Ezra Pound admitted an influence, but wished Whitman was not so uncouth; D.H. Lawrence may have been the first to register the perennial quibble that in attempting to embrace all the world, Whitman had sacrificed the individual will which drives one to particular things. William Carlos Williams acclaimed Whitman mainly to antagonize Eliot and his followers. Most of the writers, like the critics, are incapable of accepting Whitman without misgivings.

It was in the 1950's—the centennial decade of *Leaves of Grass*—that a sustained scholarly reevaluation of Whitman occurred. Two exhaustive critical biographies, Allen's *The Solitary Singer* (1955) and Roger Asselineau's *The Evolution of Walt Whitman* (1954, trans. 1960, 1962), at last attempted to present the poet in full, free of broad generalizations and uninterrogated assumptions. Richard Chase, Charles Feidelson, Jr., and Miller contributed large-scale critical works on Whitman during this time.

One of the most important texts of the Whitman revival, however, came from the poet-critic Randall Jarrell. His funny, impassioned, highly readable essay "Some Lines from Whitman" (1952) identifies a trend toward appropriating Whitman as a writer of visionary ideas conveyed in lamentably crude poetry. But Jarrell disagrees with this development; for him, Whitman is "a poet of the greatest and oddest delicacy and originality and sensitivity, so far as words are concerned" (Jarrell 99). Even Whitman's worst lines—and Jarrell grants that, as with any great poet, there are many—are interesting for being so spectacularly and weirdly bad. They only provide further grounds for appreciating Whitman the wordsmith, since "only a man with the most extraordinary feel for language ... could have cooked up Whitman's worst messes" (Jarrell 101). Jarrell thinks "Song of Myself" Whitman's greatest effort, and it is from that poem that he pulls a host of lines for which Whitman ranks among the most subtle and inventive of poets, among them: "my gore dribs, thinn'd with the ooze of my skin," "Flaunt of the sunshine I need not your bask—lie over!" "I effuse my flesh in eddies, and drift it in lacy jags," and "look in my face while I snuff the sidle of evening." And all these lines are joined in an utterly original logic of "likeness and opposition and continuation and climax and anti-climax" (Jarrell 104). Whitman's texts were "well-made" poems after all. In the end, Jarrell laments the fact that he has been forced to state the obvious in defending the great poet against the "baby critics" who fail to appreciate or understand him.

Another seminal essay of the era was Malcolm Cowley's introduction to the 1959 reissue of the first *Leaves of Grass*. Cowley considers the 1855 *Leaves*, and particularly "Song of Myself," to be Whitman's best work, the "buried masterpiece of American writing." Moreover, though he enumerates the traditionally-recognized sources of the poem (Emerson, Italian opera, George Sand, Frances Wright, Egyptology and astronomy, etc.), Cowley believes that "Song of Myself" is mistakenly read as the sum of these sources, or a kind of report on 1850's popular culture. But in fact the true sources of the poem are works and authors like the *Bhagavad-Gita*, William Blake, Rimbaud, and Nietzsche. That Rimbaud was *born* in 1854 is beside the point; for Cowley (and here he shows his own predisposition) the connection lies in an affinity for mysticism and prophecy occasioned in most instances by ecstatic experiences:

> The poem is hardly at all concerned with American nationalism, political democracy, contemporary progress, or other social themes that are commonly associated with Whitman's work. The "incomparable things" that Emerson found in it are philosophical and religious principles. Its subject is a state of illumination induced by two (or three) separate moments of ecstasy. In more or less narrative sequence it describes those moments, their sequels in life, and the doctrines to which they give rise. The doctrines are not expounded by logical steps or supported by arguments; instead they are presented dramatically, that is, as the new convictions of a hero, and they are revealed by successive unfoldings of his states of mind. (Cowley xiv-xv)

Thus "Song of Myself" is structured in two ways: as an associative progression unified by its ecstatic tone; and as a narrative of enlightenment (Cowley later breaks this narrative into nine parts). Though Cowley believes that Whitman espoused a coherent philosophy best understood as similar to certain Eastern thought, he does not believe "Song of Myself" is to be read as an essay or argument. Cowley's essay sets in motion two hardy critical constructs: the revitalized figure of Whitman-as-mystic (just in time for the 60's), and the search for the elusive structure of "Song of Myself" (a kind of Whitman genome project).

It is worth mentioning an early essay on the political aspects of Whitman—"Whitman and Melville" (1950) by the Marxist critic C.L.R. James—because it issues a surprising challenge to Whitman's professed democratic ideology. James allows that Whitman is a great lyric Romantic poet, and even that free verse is a uniquely democratic form, but he echoes Lawrence in finding Whitman's all-embracing rhetoric unconvincing: "But one who is one with everybody is one with nobody" (James 204). James finds Whitman's thralldom to the progressive ideals of Industry and Science disturbing, warning that "this writing of Whitman's was exactly what a skillful publicist on their behalf would have written—visionary ideals of individual freedom and concrete subordination to the reality of the prevailing regime" (James 205). The same blindness applies to Whitman's cult of the body; "[Whitman's] 'body beautiful,' 'body electric,' and 'seminal wetness' are the reservoir from which advertisers of foods, toothpaste, vitamins, deodorants, draw an unending source of inspiration by which to cheat and corrupt the American people" (James 206). For James, Whitman is the dupe of a rhetorical construct in which America in itself automatically signifies rebellion. Finally, Whitman compares unfavorably to Melville because while Whitman pays lip-service to the working class from the comfortable perch of his ultimately elitist ideology, Melville "described with absolute precision various individuals in their social setting, the work they did, their relations with other men" (James 209). Melville understands the price that modernity will pay for industrialization and sentimentalized individuality.

Such resurrections and contestations inaugurated the field of Whitman studies, in which scolars like Milton Hindus, Arthur Golden, Ed Folsom, Alan Trachtenberg, and M. Wynn Thomas proceeded to reevaluate assumptions about Whitman; to pursue a deeper understanding of the structures and language of his poems; to place

Whitman in conversation with other American writers; to situate Whitman in world literature and trace his international influence; to gather and contextualize further biographical and historical details pertaining to the poet and his times; and to generate scholarly editions of his work. Justin Kaplan's biography *Walt Whitman: A Life* (1980) deals more explicitly than previous work with Whitman's homosexuality. In "Emerson, Whitman, and the Paradox of Self-Reliance" (1982), Jerome Loving utilizes Harold Bloom's theory of influence to show how Whitman's misreading of Emerson resulted in a more mature poetry than "The Poet" could authorize on its own. In an entry on Whitman for the book *American Literature to 1900* (1987), Denis Donoghue finds Whitman too divided to be the potential shill for capitalist ideology that C.L.R. James had once envisioned (and Jarrell, too, is still present in Donoghue, who also finds Whitman's linguistic sensibility "delicate"). David Leverenz, in *Manhood and the American Renaissance* (1989), gives his reader a running commentary of his own reactions as he reads Whitman and responds as the "you" being addressed.

The centennial of Whitman's death saw an explosion of new discourse (Whitman, like America itself, is celebrated at his milestones). Recent criticism has been particularly concerned with Whitman's critical history, with looking at previously-neglected texts, and with the application of theory from the perspective of gender studies, queer theory, new historicism, performance studies, and American studies.

Harold Aspiz and James Perrin Warren, in "The Body Politic in *Democratic Vistas*" (1994) and "Reading Whitman's Postwar Poetry" (1995), respectively, identify Whitman's use of contemporary evolutionary models of thought (such as Darwin's) to envision the parallel development of bodies, poems, and the nation. Louis Simpson and David S. Reynolds historicize Whitman's writing about sexuality. Simpson's "Strategies of Sex in Whitman's Poetry" (1994) shows how Whitman's ambiguous language would have signified acceptable male friendship to many readers, while simultaneously being decoded, by those in the know, as treating homosexual themes. Reynolds's "Whitman and Nineteenth-Century Views of Gender and Sexuality" (1994) illustrates the way in which Whitman reacted to both the prudish moral novels and the lascivious erotic literature of his period by adopting the tropes of modern science and religious movements to create a sanitized and spiritualized eroticism.

Betsy Erkkila, in "Whitman and the Homosexual Republic" (1994), begins by quoting a letter from Cowley to Kenneth Burke in which Cowley says of Whitman, "Very strange amalgam he made between cocksucking and democracy." Her view is that, in spite of its existence, no one has acknowledged that there is any "amalgam" at all; early critics covered up or explained away Whitman's homosexuality, and later critics kept it separate from the issue of Whitman's politics. But, as Erkkila points out, affection between men was political for Whitman, and "the languages of sexuality and spirituality, same-sex love and love between men and women, private and public, intersect and flow into each other in Whitman's work" (Erkkila 158). Thus, "the democratic knowledge that the poet receives of an entire universe bathed in an erotic force that links men, women, God, and the natural world in a vision of mystic unity is associated with sexual and bodily ecstasy, an ecstasy that is included but is not limited to the pleasures of cocksucking between men" (Erkkila has appropriated Cowley's term "cocksucking" to describe an actual act which, unlike "homosexuality," is not a social/historical construct) (Erkkila 158). In other words, sexuality is political, but its categories are not monolithic and thus cannot be put in a one-to-one relationship with a particular political position.

Tom Yingling argues along the same lines in his essay "Homosexuality and Utopian Discourse in American Poetry" (1996), pointing out that many gay American poets have had to negotiate the apparently antithetical relationship between homosexuality and American utopianism; indeed, the former has often been construed as a threat to the latter. However, Yingling reads Whitman and others as actually constructing a utopianism *from* their understanding of homosexuality as a model of social freedom. Utopias, Yingling contends, arise from "moments of vision in which is imagined an alternative social organization"—and this imagination requires the loosening of the codes of signification that one finds in both sexuality and poetry (Yingling 145). Vivian Pollak is perhaps somewhat less convinced in "Whitman's Visionary Feminism" (1996), in which she traces Whitman's ambivalence between sometimes radical and sometimes utterly conventional, or even reactionary, positions in regard to both gender and race.

In "'As If I Were With You'—The Performance of Whitman's Poetry," Stephen Railton assesses the effect of Whitman's use of the second-person pronoun "more pervasively than any other major poet." The topic has a history (C. Carroll Hollis had called the address to the reader Whitman's "illocutionary stance;" for Ezra Greenspan it was the "vocative technique"), but for Railton it points to the performative aspect of Whitman's poems. In fact, Whitman rarely read for an audience, but Railton contends that Whitman nevertheless postulated an actual reader and conceived of his poems as public and dramatic. This argument allows Railton to make several interesting claims: first among these is that the "you" is necessary in preventing a poem like "Song of Myself" from being pure solipsism, since the reader is actually outside of the poet's universe which contains everything else. The performance also solves the problem of structure in "Song of Myself":

> "Song of Myself is not a poem about "what happened"; instead, the poem itself, like any performance, is what is happening as it is being read. That is the when of the poem: the "this day and night" the reader spends with the poet, reading the poem …The dramatically charged space between Whitman and the reader is the where of the poem. The poem doesn't have a plot; it is a plot—it is organized around the reader, whose assumptions Whitman seeks to make over in his own image. (Railton 9)

The poem is a strategy, or a transaction. The "you" also allows Whitman to remain ambivalent about readerly acceptance of his sexuality; to reimagine "the trope of poetic immortality" in "Crossing Brooklyn Ferry;" and to establish a direct, erotic relationship with the reader who holds him when he holds his book.

As James E. Miller, Jr. once pointed out, Whitman must be accepted or rejected by every American poet. He has influenced such diverse writers as Wallace Stevens, Allen Ginsberg, Jorge Luis Borges, Henry Miller, Langston Hughes, Pablo Neruda, Muriel Rukeyser, and Milton Kessler. But an opinion on Whitman and a recognition of his influence extends to other artists as well, and to critics, and to readers, and to anyone who thinks about the nation that Whitman made himself inseparable from along with the ideals—naive, subversive, erotic, loving, fleeting, and eternal—that live and speak to us in his poems.

Works Cited

Allen, Gay Wilson. *The Solitary Singer: A Critical Biography of Walt Whitman*. New York: New York University Press, 1967 (first pub. 1955).

Aspiz, Harold. "The Body Politic in *Democratic Vistas*." In *Walt Whitman: The Centennial Essays*, ed. by Ed Folsom. Iowa City: University of Iowa Press, 1994.

Cather, Willa. "['sometimes sublime, sometimes ridiculous']." In *Critical Essays on Walt Whitman*, ed. by James Woodress. Boston: G.K. Hall, 1983.

Christian Examiner 60. Review of *Leaves of Grass*. In *Walt Whitman: The Contemporary Reviews*, ed. by Kenneth M. Price. Cambridge: Cambridge University Press, 1996.

Conway, Moncure D. Review of *Leaves of Grass*. In *Walt Whitman: The Contemporary Reviews*, ed. by Kenneth M. Price. Cambridge: Cambridge University Press, 1996.

Cowley, Malcolm. "Editor's Introduction." In *Walt Whitman's* Leaves of Grass: *The First (1855) Edition*. New York: The Viking Press, 1959.

Daily Times. Review of *Leaves of Grass*. In *Walt Whitman: The Contemporary Reviews*, ed. by Kenneth M. Price. Cambridge: Cambridge University Press, 1996.

Dana, Charles A. "New Publications: *Leaves of Grass*." In *Walt Whitman: The Contemporary Reviews*, ed. by Kenneth M. Price. Cambridge: Cambridge University Press, 1996.

Donoghue, Denis. "Walt Whitman." In *American Literature to 1900*, ed. by Marcus Cunliffe. New York: Peter Bedrick Books, 1987.

Emerson, Ralph Waldo. *Essays: First and Second Series*. New York: Vintage Books, 1990.

Erkkila, Betsy. "Whitman and the Homosexual Republic." In *Walt Whitman: The Centennial Essays*, ed. by Ed Folsom. Iowa City: University of Iowa Press, 1994.

Fern, Fanny. "Fresh Fern Leaves: Leaves of Grass." In *Walt Whitman: The Contemporary Reviews*, ed. by Kenneth M. Price. Cambridge: Cambridge University Press, 1996.

Gilchrist, Anne. "An Englishwoman's Estimate of Walt Whitman." In *Critical Essays on Walt Whitman*, ed. by James Woodress. Boston: G.K. Hall, 1983.

Griswold, Rufus W. Review of *Leaves of Grass*. In *Walt Whitman: The Contemporary Reviews*, ed. by Kenneth M. Price. Cambridge: Cambridge University Press, 1996.

Hale, Edward Everett. Review of *Leaves of Grass*. In *Walt Whitman: The Contemporary Reviews*, ed. by Kenneth M. Price. Cambridge: Cambridge University Press, 1996.

Howells, William Dean. "[A Young Novelist Fails to Appreciate *Drum-Taps*]." In *Critical Essays on Walt Whitman*, ed. by James Woodress. Boston: G.K. Hall, 1983.

James, C.L.R. "Whitman and Melville." In *The C.L.R. James Reader*, ed. by Anna Grimshaw. Cambridge, Mass.: Blackwell, 1992.

James, Henry. "[Another Fledgling Novelist Disparages *Drum-Taps*]." In *Critical Essays on Walt Whitman*, ed. by James Woodress. Boston: G.K. Hall, 1983.

James, William. "The Religion of Healthy-Mindedness." In *Critical Essays on Walt Whitman*, ed. by James Woodress. Boston: G.K. Hall, 1983.

Jarrell, Randall. "Some Lines from Whitman." In *No Other Book: Selected Essays*. New York: HarperCollins, 1999.

Leverenz, David. *Manhood and the American Renaissance*. Ithaca: Cornell University Press, 1989.

Loving, Jerome. "Emerson, Whitman, and the Paradox of Self-Reliance." In *Critical Essays on Walt Whitman*, ed. by James Woodress. Boston: G.K. Hall, 1983.

Lawrence, D.H. "Whitman." In *Critical Essays on Walt Whitman*, ed. by James Woodress. Boston: G.K. Hall, 1983.

Miller, James E., Jr. "The Care and Feeding of American Long Poems: The American Epic from Barlow to Berryman." In *Critical Essays on Walt Whitman*, ed. by James Woodress. Boston: G.K. Hall, 1983.

Norton, Charles Eliot. "Whitman's *Leaves of Grass*." In *Walt Whitman: The Contemporary Reviews*, ed. by Kenneth M. Price. Cambridge: Cambridge University Press, 1996.

Pollak, Vivian R. "'In Loftiest Spheres': Whitman's Visionary Feminism." In *Breaking Bounds: Whitman and American Cultural Studies*, ed. by Betsy Erkkila and Jay Grossman. New York: Oxford University Press, 1996.

Pound, Ezra. "What I Feel about Walt Whitman." In *Critical Essays on Walt Whitman*, ed. by James Woodress. Boston: G.K. Hall, 1983.

Railton, Stephen. "'As If I Were With You'—The Performance of Whitman's Poetry." In *The Cambridge Companion to Walt Whitman*, ed. by Ezra Greenspan. Cambridge: Cambridge University Press, 1995.

Reynolds, David S. "Whitman and Nineteenth-Century Views of Gender and Sexuality." In *Walt Whitman of Mickle Street: A Centennial Collection*, ed. by Geoffrey M. Sill. Knoxville: The University of Tennessee Press, 1994.

Rossetti, William Michael. "[Whitman's English Editor Writes a Friend]." In *Critical Essays on Walt Whitman*, ed. by James Woodress. Boston: G.K. Hall, 1983.

Simpson, Louis. "Strategies of Sex in Whitman's Poetry." In *Walt Whitman of Mickle Street: A Centennial Collection*, ed. by Geoffrey M. Sill. Knoxville: The University of Tennessee Press, 1994.

Swinburne, Algernon Charles. "Whitmania." In *Critical Essays on Walt Whitman*, ed. by James Woodress. Boston: G.K. Hall, 1983.

Thoreau, Henry David. "[A Letter about Whitman]." In *Critical Essays on Walt Whitman*, ed. by James Woodress. Boston: G.K. Hall, 1983.

Warren, James Perrin. "Reading Whitman's Postwar Poetry." In *The Cambridge Companion to Walt Whitman*, ed. by Ezra Greenspan. Cambridge: Cambridge University Press, 1995.

Whitman, Walt. "Walt Whitman and His Poems." In *Walt Whitman: The Contemporary Reviews*, ed. by Kenneth M. Price. Cambridge: Cambridge University Press, 1996.

———. *Walt Whitman: Poetry and Prose*. New York: The Library of America, 1996.

Wilde, Oscar. "The Gospel According to Walt Whitman." In *Walt Whitman: The Contemporary Reviews*, ed. by Kenneth M. Price. Cambridge: Cambridge University Press, 1996.

Williams, William Carlos. "An Essay on *Leaves of Grass*." In Leaves of Grass: *One Hundred Years After*, ed. by Milton Hindus. Stanford: Stanford University Press, 1955.

Yingling, Tom. "Homosexuality and Utopian Discourse in American Poetry." In *Breaking Bounds: Whitman and American Cultural Studies*, ed. by Betsy Erkkila and Jay Grossman. New York: Oxford University Press, 1996.

RANDALL JARRELL

Some Lines From Whitman

Whitman, Dickinson, and Melville seem to me the best poets of the nineteenth century here in America. Melville's poetry has been grotesquely underestimated, but of course it is only in the last four or five years that it has been much read; in the long run, in spite of the awkwardness and amateurishness of so much of it, it will surely be thought well of. (In the short run it will probably be thought entirely too well of. Melville is a great poet only in the prose of *Moby Dick*.) Dickinson's poetry has been thoroughly read, and well though undifferentiatingly loved—after a few decades or centuries almost everybody will be able to see through Dickinson to her poems. But something odd has happened to the living changing part of Whitman's reputation: nowadays it is people who are not particularly interested in poetry, people who say that they read a poem for what it says, not for how it says it, who admire Whitman most. Whitman is often written about, either approvingly or disapprovingly, as if he were the Thomas Wolfe of nineteenth-century democracy, the hero of a De Mille movie about Walt Whitman. (People even talk about a war in which Walt Whitman and Henry James chose up sides, to begin with, and in which you and I will go on fighting till the day we die.) All this sort of thing, and all the bad poetry that there of course is in Whitman—for any poet has written enough bad poetry to scare away anybody—has helped to

From *No Other Book: Selected Essays*. © 1999 Harper Collins. Reprinted by permission.

scare away from Whitman most "serious readers of modern poetry." They do not talk of his poems, as a rule, with any real liking or knowledge. Serious readers, people who are ashamed of not knowing all Hopkins by heart, are not at all ashamed to say, "I don't really know Whitman very well." This may harm Whitman in your eyes, they know, but that is a chance that poets have to take. Yet "their" Hopkins, that good critic and great poet, wrote about Whitman, after seeing five or six of his poems in a newspaper, review: "I may as well say what I should not otherwise have said, that I always knew in my heart Walt Whitman's mind to be more like my own than any other man's living. As he is a very great scoundrel this is not a very pleasant confession." And Henry James, the leader of "their" side in that awful imaginary war of which I spoke, once read Whitman to Edith Wharton (much as Mozart used to imitate, on the piano, the organ) with such power and solemnity that both sat shaken and silent; it was after this reading that James expressed his regret at Whitman's "too extensive acquaintance with the foreign languages." Almost all the most "original and advanced" poets and critics and readers of the last part of the nineteenth century thought Whitman as original and advanced as themselves, in manner as well as in matter. Can Whitman really be a sort of Thomas Wolfe or Carl Sandburg or Robinson Jeffers or Henry Miller—or a sort of Balzac of poetry, whose every part is crude but whose whole is somehow great? He is not, nor could he be; a poem, like Pope's spider, "lives along the line," and all the dead lines in the world will not make one live poem. As Blake says, "all sublimity is founded on minute discrimination," and it is in these "minute particulars" of Blake's that any poem has its primary existence.

To show Whitman for what he is one does not need to praise or explain or argue, one needs simply to quote. He himself said, "I and mine do not convince by arguments, similes, rhymes, / We convince, by our presence." Even a few of his phrases are enough to show us that Whitman was no sweeping rhetorician, but a poet of the greatest and oddest delicacy and originality and sensitivity, so far as words are concerned. This is, after all, the poet who said, "Blind loving wrestling touch, sheath'd hooded sharp-tooth'd touch"; who said, "Smartly attired, countenance smiling, form upright, death under the breast-bones, hell under the skull-bones"; who said, "Agonies are one of my changes of garments"; who saw grass as the "flag of my disposition," saw "the sharp-peak'd farmhouse, with its scallop'd scum and slender shoots from the gutters," heard a plane's "wild ascending lisp," and saw and heard how at the amputation "what is removed drops horribly in a pail." This is the poet for whom the sea was "howler and scooper of storms," reaching out to us with "crooked inviting fingers"; who went "leaping chasms with a pike-pointed staff, clinging to topples of brittle and blue"; who, a runaway slave, saw how "my gore dribs, thinn'd with the ooze of my skin"; who went "lithographing Kronos ... buying drafts of Osiris"; who stared out at the "little plentiful mannikins skipping around in collars and tail'd coats, / I am aware who they are, (they are positively not worms or fleas)." For he is, at his best, beautifully witty: he says gravely, "I find I incorporate gneiss, coals, long-threaded moss, fruits, grain, esculent roots, / And am stucco'd with quadrupeds and birds all over"; and of these quadrupeds and birds "not one is respectable or unhappy over the whole earth." He calls advice: "Unscrew the locks from the doors! Unscrew the doors from their jambs!" He publishes the results of research: "Having pried through the strata, analyz'd to a hair, counsel'd with doctors and calculated close, / I find no sweeter fat than sticks to my own bones." Everybody remembers how he told the Muse to "cross out please those immensely overpaid accounts, / That matter of Troy and Achilles' wrath, and Aeneas', Odysseus' wanderings," but his account of the arrival of the "illustrious emigré" here in the New World is even better: "Bluff'd not a bit by drainpipe, gasometer, artificial fertilizers, / Smiling and pleas'd with palpable intent to stay, / She's here, install'd amid the kitchenware." Or he sees, like another Bruegel, "the mechanic's wife with the babe at her nipple interceding for every person born, / Three scythes at harvest whizzing in a row from three lusty angels with shirts bagg'd out at their waists, / The snag-toothed hostler with red hair redeeming sins past and to come"—the passage has enough wit not only (in Johnson's phrase) to keep it sweet, but enough to make it believable. He says:

I project my hat, sit shame-faced, and beg.

Enough! Enough! Enough!
Somehow I have been stunn'd. Stand back!
Give me a little time beyond my cuff'd head, slumbers,
                                    dreams, gaping,
I discover myself on the verge of a usual mistake.

There is in such changes of tone as these the essence of wit. And Whitman is even more farfetched than he is witty; he can say about Doubters, in the most improbable and explosive of juxtapositions: "I know every one of you, I know the sea of torment, doubt, despair and unbelief. / How the flukes splash! How they contort rapid as lightning, with splashes and spouts of blood!" Who else would have said about God: "As the hugging and loving bed-fellow sleeps at my side through the night, and withdraws at the break of day with stealthy, tread, / Leaving me baskets cover'd with white towels, swelling the house with their plenty"?—the Psalmist himself, his cup running over, would have looked at Whitman with dazzled eyes. (Whitman was persuaded by friends to hide the fact that it was God he was talking about.) He says, "Flaunt of the sunshine I need not your bask—lie over!" This unusual employment of verbs is usual enough in participle-loving Whitman, who also asks you to "look in my face while I snuff the sidle of evening," or tells you, "I effuse my flesh in eddies, and drift it in lacy jags." Here are some typical beginnings of poems: "City of orgies, walks, and joys ... Not heaving from ribb'd breast only ... O take my hand Walt Whitman! Such gliding wonders! Such sights and sounds! Such join'd unended links ..." He says to the objects of the world, "You have waited, you always wait, you dumb, beautiful ministers"; sees "the sun and stars that float in the open air, / The apple-shaped earth"; says, "O suns— O grass of graves— O perpetual transfers and promotions, / If you do not say anything how can I say anything?" Not many poets have written better, in queerer and more convincing and more individual language, about the world's *gliding wonders*: the phrase seems particularly right for Whitman. He speaks of those "circling rivers the breath," of the "savage old mother incessantly crying, / To the boy's soul's questions sullenly timing, some drown'd secret hissing"—ends a poem, once, "We have voided all but freedom and our own joy." How can one quote enough? If the reader thinks that all this is like Thomas Wolfe he *is* Thomas Wolfe; nothing else could explain it. Poetry like this is as far as possible from the work of any ordinary rhetorician, whose phrases cascade over us like suds of the oldest and most-advertised detergent.

The interesting thing about Whitman's worst language (for, just as few poets have ever written better, few poets have ever written worse) is how unusually absurd, how really ingeniously bad, such language is. I will quote none of the most famous examples; but even a line like *O culpable! I acknowledge. I exposé!* is not anything that you and I could do—only a man with the most extraordinary feel for language, or none whatsoever, could have cooked up Whitman's worst messes. For instance: what other man in all the history of this planet would have said, "I am a habitan of Vienna"? (One has an immediate vision of him as a sort of French-Canadian halfbreed to whom the Viennese are offering, with trepidation, through the bars of a zoological garden, little mounds of whipped cream.) And *enclaircise*—why, it's as bad as *explicate*! We are right to resent his having made up his own horrors, instead of sticking to the ones that we ourselves employ. But when Whitman says, "I dote on myself, there is that lot of me and all so luscious," we should realize that we are not the only ones who are amused. And the queerly bad and merely queer and queerly good will often change into one another without warning: "Hefts of the moving world, at innocent gambols silently rising, freshly exuding, / Scooting obliquely high and low"—not good, but *queer*!—suddenly becomes, "Something I cannot see puts up libidinous prongs, / Seas of bright juice suffuse heaven," and it is sunrise.

But it is not in individual lines and phrases, but in passages of some length, that Whitman is at his best. In the following quotation Whitman has something difficult to express, something that there are many formulas, all bad, for expressing; he expresses it with complete success, in language of the most dazzling originality:

> The orchestra whirls me wider than Uranus flies,
> It wrenches such ardors from me I did not know I possess'd them,
> It sails me, I dab with bare feet, they are lick'd by the indolent waves,
> I am cut by bitter and angry hail, I lose my breath,
> Steep'd amid honey'd morphine, my windpipe throttled in fakes of
>   death,
> At length let up again to feel the puzzle of puzzles,
> And that we call Being.

One hardly knows what to point at—everything works. But *wrenches* and *did not know I possess'd them*; the incredible *it sails me, I dab with bare feet, lick'd by the indolent, steep'd amid honey'd morphine; my windpipe throttled in fakes of death*—no wonder Crane admired Whitman! This originality, as absolute in its way as that of Berlioz's orchestration, is often at Whitman's command:

I am a dance—play up there! the fit is whirling me fast!
I am the ever-laughing—it is new moon and twilight,
I see the hiding of douceurs, I see nimble ghosts whichever way I look,
Cache and cache again deep in the ground and sea, and where it is
    neither ground nor sea.
Well do they do their jobs those journeymen divine,
Only from me can they hide nothing, and would not if they could,
I reckon I am their boss and they make me a pet besides,
And surround me and lead me and run ahead when I walk,
To lift their sunning covers to signify me with stretch'd arms, and
    resume the way;
Onward we move, a gay gang of blackguards! with mirth-shouting
    music and wild-flapping pennants of joy!

If you did not believe Hopkins's remark about Whitman, that *gay gang of blackguards* ought to shake you. Whitman shares Hopkins's passion for "dappled" effects, but he slides in and out of them with ambiguous swiftness. And he has at his command a language of the calmest and most prosaic reality, one that seems to do no more than present:

The little one sleeps in its cradle.
I lift the gauze and look a long time, and silently brush away flies with
    my hand.
The youngster and the red-faced girl turn aside up the bushy hill,
I peeringly view them from the top.

The suicide sprawls on the bloody floor of the bedroom.
I witness the corpse with its dabbled hair, I note where the pistol has
    fallen.

It is like magic: that is, something has been done to us without our knowing how it was done; but if we look at the lines again we see the *gauze, silently, youngster, red-faced, bushy, peeringly, dabbled*—not that this is all we see. "Present! present!" said James; these are presented, put down side by side to form a little "view of life," from the cradle to the last bloody floor of the bedroom. Very often the things presented form nothing but a list:

The pure contralto sings in the organ loft,
The carpenter dresses his plank, the tongue of his foreplane whistles
its wild ascending lisp,
The married and unmarried children ride home to their Thanksgiving
dinner,
The pilot seizes the king-pin, he heaves down with a strong arm,
The mate stands braced in the whale-boat, lance and harpoon are
ready,
The duck-shooter walks by silent and cautious stretches,
The deacons are ordain'd with cross'd hands at the altar,
The spinning-girl retreats and advances, to the hum of the big wheel,
The farmer stops by the bars as he walks on a First-day loafe and looks
at the oats and rye,
The lunatic is carried at last to the asylum a confirm'd case,
(He will never sleep any more as he did in the cot in his mother's bed-
room;)
The jour printer with gray head and gaunt jaws works at his case,
He turns his quid of tobacco while his eyes blur with the manuscript,
The malform'd limbs are tied to the surgeon's table,
What is removed drops horribly in a pail ...

It is only a list—but what a list! And how delicately, in what different
ways—likeness and opposition and continuation and climax and
anticlimax—the transitions are managed, whenever Whitman wants to
manage them. Notice them in the next quotation, another "mere list":

The bride unrumples her white dress, the minute-hand of the clock
moves slowly,
The opium-eater reclines with rigid head and just-open'd lips,
The prostitute draggles her shawl, her bonnet bobs on her tipsy and
pimpled neck ...

The first line is joined to the third by *unrumples* and *draggles*, *white dress*
and *shawl*; the second to the third by *rigid head*, *bobs*, *tipsy*, *neck*; the first
to the second by *slowly*, *just-open'd*, and the slowing-down of time in both
states. And occasionally one of these lists is metamorphosed into
something we have no name for; the man who would call the next
quotation a mere list—anybody will feel this—would boil his babies up
for soap:

Ever the hard unsunk ground,
Ever the eaters and drinkers, ever the upward and downward sun,
Ever myself and my neighbors, refreshing, wicked, real,
Ever the old inexplicable query, ever that thorned thumb, that breath
     of itches and thirsts,
Ever the vexer's hoot! hoot! till we find where the sly one hides and
     bring him forth,
Ever the sobbing liquid of life,
Ever the bandage under the chin, ever the trestles of death.

Sometimes Whitman will take what would generally be considered
an unpromising subject (in this case, a woman peeping at men in bathing
naked) and treat it with such tenderness and subtlety and understanding
that we are ashamed of ourselves for having thought it unpromising, and
murmur that Chekhov himself couldn't have treated it better:

Twenty-eight young men bathe by the shore,
Twenty-eight young men and all so friendly,
Twenty-eight years of womanly life and all so lonesome.

She owns the fine house by the rise of the bank,
She hides handsome and richly drest aft the blinds of the window.

Which of the young men does she like the best?
Ah the homeliest of them is beautiful to her.

Where are you off to, lady? for I see you,
You splash in the water there, yet stay stock still in your room.
Dancing and laughing along the beach came the twenty-ninth
     bather,
The rest did not see her, but she saw them and loved them.

The beards of the young men glistened with wet, it ran from their
     long hair,
Little streams pass'd all over their bodies.

An unseen hand also pass'd over their bodies,
It descended tremblingly from their temples and ribs.

The young men float on their backs, their white bellies bulge to the
     sun, they do not ask who seizes fast to them,
They do not know who puffs and declines with pendant and bending
     arch,
They do not know whom they souse with spray.

   And in the same poem (that "Song of Myself" in which one finds
half his best work) the writer can say of a sea-fight:

Stretched and still lies the midnight,
Two great hulls motionless on the breast of the darkness,
Our vessel riddled and slowly sinking, preparations to pass to the one
     we have conquer'd,
The captain on the quarter-deck coldly giving his orders through a
     countenance white as a sheet,
Near by the corpse of the child that serv'd in the cabin,
The dead face of an old salt with long white hair and carefully curl'd
     whiskers,
The flames spite of all that can be done flickering aloft and below,
The husky voices of the two or three officers yet fit for duty,
Formless stacks of bodies and bodies by themselves, dabs of flesh upon
     the masts and spars,
Cut of cordage, dangle of rigging, slight shock of the soothe of waves,
Black and impassive guns, litter of powder-parcels, strong scent,
A few large stars overhead, silent and mournful shining,
Delicate snuffs of sea-breeze, smells of sedgy grass and fields by the
     shore, death-messages given in charge to survivors,
The hiss of the surgeon's knife, the gnawing teeth of his saw,
Wheeze, cluck, swash of falling blood, short wild scream, and long,
     dull, tapering groan,
These so, these irretrievable.

There are faults in this passage, and they *do not matter*: the serious truth,
the complete realization of these last lines make us remember that few
poets have shown more of the tears of things, and the joy of things, and
of the reality beneath either tears or joy. Even Whitman's most general
or political statements sometimes are good: everybody knows his
"When liberty goes out of a place it is not the first to go, nor the second

or third to go, / It waits for all the rest to go, it is the last"; these
sentences about the United States just before the Civil War may be less
familiar:

> Are those really Congressmen? are those the great Judges? is that the
>   President?
> Then I will sleep awhile yet, for I see that these States sleep, for
>   reasons;
> (With gathering murk, with muttering thunder and lambent shoots we
>   all duly awake,
> South, North, East, West, inland and seaboard, we will surely awake.)

How well, with what firmness and dignity and command, Whitman does
such passages! And Whitman's doubts that he has done them or anything
else well—ah, there is nothing he does better:

> The best I had done seemed to me blank and suspicious,
> My great thoughts as I supposed them, were they not in reality
>   meagre?
> I am he who knew what it was to be evil,
> I too knitted the old knot of contrariety ...
> Saw many I loved in the street or ferry-boat or public assembly, yet
>   never told them a word,
> Lived the same life with the rest, the same old laughing, gnawing,
>   sleeping,
> Played the part that still looks back on the actor and actress,
> The same old role, the role that is what we make it ...

Whitman says once that the "look of the bay mare shames silliness
out of me." This is true—sometimes it is true; but more often the
silliness and affection and cant and exaggeration are there shamelessly,
the Old Adam that was in Whitman from the beginning and the awful
new one that he created to keep it company. But as he says, "I know
perfectly well my own egotism, / Know my omnivorous lines and must
not write any less." He says over and over that there are in him good and
bad, wise and foolish, anything at all and its antonym, and he is telling
the truth; there is in him almost everything in the world, so that one
responds to him, willingly or unwillingly, almost as one does to the

world, that world which makes the hairs of one's flesh stand up, which seems both evil beyond any rejection and wonderful beyond any acceptance. We cannot help seeing that there is something absurd about any judgment we make of its whole—for there is no "point of view" at which we can stand to make the judgment, and the moral categories that mean most to us seem no more to apply to its whole than our spatial or temporal or causal categories seem to apply to its beginning or its end. (But we need no arguments to make our judgments seem absurd—we feel their absurdity without argument.) In some like sense Whitman is a world, a waste with, here and there, systems blazing at random out of the darkness. Only an innocent and rigidly methodical mind will reject it for this disorganization particularly since there are in it, here and there, little systems as beautifully and astonishingly organized as the rings and satellites of Saturn:

> I understand the large hearts of heroes,
> The courage of present times and all times,
> How the skipper saw the crowded and rudderless wreck of the steam-
>   ship, and Death chasing it up and down the storm,
> How he knuckled tight and gave not back an inch, and was faithful of
>   days and faithful of nights,
> And chalked in large letters on a board, Be of good cheer, we will not
>   desert you;
> How he follow'd with them and tack'd with them three days and
>   would not give it up,
> How he saved the drifting company at last,
> How the lank loose-gown'd women looked when boated from the side
>   of their prepared graves,
> How the silent old-faced infants and the lifted sick, and the sharp-
>   lipp'd unshaved men;
> All this I swallow, it tastes good, I like it well, it becomes mine,
> I am the man, I suffered, I was there.

In the last lines of this quotation Whitman has reached—as great writers always reach—a point at which criticism seems not only unnecessary but absurd: these lines are so good that even admiration feels like insolence, and one is ashamed of anything that one can find to say about them. How anyone can dismiss or accept patronizingly the man who wrote them, I do not understand.

The enormous and apparent advantages of form, of omission and selection, of the highest degree of organization, are accompanied by important disadvantages—and there are far greater works than *Leaves of Grass* to make us realize this. But if we compare Whitman with that very beautiful poet Alfred Tennyson, the most skillful of all Whitman's contemporaries, we are at once aware of how limiting Tennyson's forms have been, of how much Tennyson has had to leave out, even in those discursive poems where he is trying to put everything in. Whitman's poems *represent* his world and himself much more satisfactorily than Tennyson's do his. In the past a few poets have both formed and represented, each in the highest degree; but in modern times what controlling, organizing, selecting poet has created a world with as much in it as Whitman's, a world that so plainly is the world? Of all modern poets he has, quantitatively speaking, "the most comprehensive soul"— and, qualitatively, a most comprehensive and comprehending one, with charities and concessions and qualifications that are rare in any time.

"Do I contradict myself? Very well then I contradict myself," wrote Whitman, as everybody remembers, and this is not naïve, or something he got from Emerson, or a complacent pose. When you organize one of the contradictory elements out of your work of art, you are getting rid not just of it, but of the contradiction of which it was a part; and it is the contradictions in works of art which make them able to represent to us— as logical and methodical generalizations cannot—our world and our selves, which are also full of contradictions. In Whitman we do not get the controlled, compressed, seemingly concordant contradictions of the great lyric poets, of a poem like, say, Hardy's "During Wind and Rain"; Whitman's contradictions are sometimes announced openly, but are more often scattered at random throughout the poems. For instance: Whitman specializes in ways of saying that there is in some sense (a very Hegelian one, generally) no evil—he says a hundred times that evil is not Real; but he also specializes in making lists of the evil of the world, lists of an unarguable reality. After his minister has recounted "the rounded catalogue divine complete," Whitman comes home and puts down what has been left out: "the countless (nineteen-twentieths) low and evil, crude and savage ... the barren soil, the evil men, the slag and hideous rot." He ends another such catalogue with the plain unexcusing "All these—all meanness and agony without end I sitting look out upon, / See, hear, and am silent." Whitman offered himself to everybody, and said brilliantly and at length what a good thing he was offering:

Sure as the most certain sure, plumb in the uprights, well entretied,
> braced in the beams,
Stout as a horse, affectionate, haughty, electrical,
I and this mystery here we stand.

Just for oddness, characteristicalness, differentness, what more could you ask in a letter of recommendation? (Whitman sounds as if he were recommending a house—haunted, but what foundations!) But after a few pages he is oddly different:

Apart from, the pulling and hauling stands what I am,
Stands amused, complacent, compassionating, idle, unitary,
Looks down, is erect; or bends an arm on an impalpable certain rest
Looking with side curved head curious what will come next,
Both in and out of the game and watching and wondering at it.

Tamburlaine is already beginning to sound like Hamlet: the employer feels uneasily, "Why, I might as well hire myself ..." And, a few pages later, Whitman puts down in ordinary-sized type, in the middle of the page, this warning to *any new person drawn toward me*:

Do you think I am trusty and faithful?
Do you see no further than this façade, this smooth and tolerant
> manner of me?
Do you suppose yourself advancing on real ground toward a real heroic
> man?
Have you no thought O dreamer that it may be all maya, illusion?

Having wonderful dreams, telling wonderful lies, was a temptation Whitman could never resist; but telling the truth was a temptation he could never resist, either. When you buy him you know what you are buying. And only an innocent and solemn and systematic mind will condemn him for his contradictions: Whitman's catalogues of evils represent realities, and his denials of their reality represent other realities, of feeling and intuition and desire. If he is faithless to logic, to Reality As It Is—whatever that is—he is faithful to the feel of things, to reality as it seems; this is all that a poet has to be faithful to, and philosophers have been known to leave logic and Reality for it.

Whitman is more coordinate and parallel than anybody, is *the* poet of parallel present participles, of twenty verbs joined by a single subject: all this helps to give his work its feeling of raw hypnotic reality, of being that world which also streams over us joined only by *ands*, until we supply the subordinating conjunctions; and since as children we see the *ands* and not the *becauses*, this method helps to give Whitman some of the freshness of childhood. How inexhaustibly interesting the world is in Whitman! Arnold all his life kept wishing that he could see the world "with a plainness as near, as flashing" as that with which Moses and Rebekah and the Argonauts saw it. He asked with elegiac nostalgia, "Who can see the green earth any more / As she was by the sources of Time?"—and all the time there was somebody alive who saw it so, as plain and near and flashing, and with a kind of calm, pastoral, Biblical dignity and elegance as well, sometimes. The *thereness* and *suchness* of the world are incarnate in Whitman as they are in few other writers.

They might have put on his tombstone WALT WHITMAN: HE HAD HIS NERVE. He is the rashest, the most inexplicable and unlikely—the most impossible, one wants to say—of poets. He somehow is in a class by himself, so that one compares him with other poets about as readily as one compares *Alice* with other books. (Even his free verse has a completely different effect from anybody else's.) Who would think of comparing him with Tennyson or Browning or Arnold or Baudelaire?—it is Homer, or the sagas, or something far away and long ago, that comes to one's mind only to be dismissed; for sometimes Whitman *is* epic, just as *Moby Dick* is, and it surprises us to be able to use truthfully this word that we have misused so many times. Whitman *is* grand, and elevated, and comprehensive, and real with an astonishing reality, and many other things—the critic points at his qualities in despair and wonder, all method failing, and simply calls them by their names. And the range of these qualities is the most extraordinary thing of all. We can surely say about him, "He was a man, take him for all in all. I shall not look upon his like again"—and wish that people had seen this and not tried to be his like: one Whitman is miracle enough, and when he comes again it will be the end of the world.

I have said so little about Whitman's faults because they are so plain: baby critics who have barely learned to complain of the lack of ambiguity in *Peter Rabbit* can tell you all that is wrong with *Leaves of Grass*. But a good many of my readers must have felt that it is ridiculous to write an essay about the obvious fact that Whitman is a great poet. It is ridiculous—just as, in 1851, it would have been ridiculous for anyone to write an essay about the obvious fact that Pope was no "classic of our prose" but a great poet. Critics have to spend half their time reiterating whatever ridiculously obvious things their age or the critics of their age have found it necessary to forget: they say despairingly, at parties, that Wordsworth is a great poet, and *won't* bore you, and tell Mr. Leavis that Milton is a great poet whose deposition *hasn't* been accomplished with astonishing ease by a few words from Eliot ... There is something essentially ridiculous about critics, anyway: what is good is good without our saying so, and beneath all our majesty we know this.

Let me finish by mentioning another quality of Whitman's—a quality, delightful to me, that I have said nothing of. If someday a tourist notices, among the ruins of New York City, a copy of *Leaves of Grass*, and stops and picks it up and reads some lines in it, she will be able to say to herself: "How very American! If he and his country had not existed, it would have been impossible to imagine them."

STEPHEN RAILTON

"As If I Were With You"—
The Performance of Whitman's Poetry

Every reader has noticed how often Walt Whitman says *I*. There are few pages of *Leaves of Grass* without at least some form of the first-person pronoun—*I, me, mine, my, myself*. Nor is there any hint of an apology in his acknowledgment of this fact: "I know perfectly well my own egotism ... and cannot say any less."[1] Yet *I* is not the pronoun that most markedly distinguishes Whitman's poetry (as C. Carroll Hollis has calculated, for example, "on a percentage basis Dickinson uses even more"[2]). *You* is. Whitman doesn't say *you* as often as he says *I*, but he does use the second-person pronoun more pervasively than any other major poet. Even the assertion of his own egotism that I've just quoted is embedded in a larger thought that reveals the interdependence of his authorial *I* and the *you* of his reader:

> I know perfectly well my own egotism,
> And know my omnivorous words, and cannot say any less,
> And would fetch you whoever you are flush with myself.

To describe this awareness of and address to the reader, Hollis borrows a term from modern linguistics and calls it Whitman's "illocutionary" stance.[3] Ezra Greenspan borrows a term from classical grammar and calls it Whitman's "vocative technique."[4] A more

From *The Cambridge Companion to Walt Whitman*, ed. by Ezra Greenspan. © 1995 Cambridge University Press.

colloquial way to indicate the crucial place *you* occupies in many of Whitman's poems is to say that they are performances. Whitman put it still more colloquially when he wrote in a notebook: "All my poems do. All I write I write to arouse in you a great personality."[5] Of course, as performances they were enacted imaginatively rather than literally. Despite Whitman's fantasies about being a national orator, speaking from real stages to packed houses, he seldom performed in front of live audiences. Even from the imaginative stage of a printed book, he was not widely read until after his death. But throughout his career he defined the goals of his poetry as public ones, and especially in the poems he wrote before the Civil War he conceived his poetry dramatically, as an address to the reader he refers to as the "listener up there" (1855, 85), the *you* reading the book. That the performance was imaginary did not matter to someone who had so impressive an imagination: What the many *you*'s establish is how real and present his reader was in Whitman's mind. *You* is what I want to explore here. What does *you* do? What is the role that Whitman's reader plays in his imagination and his poetry? Who is *you*? Can we be specific about the way he conceived his reader? And what does Whitman mean when he says that the aim of his performance is to fetch *you* flush with himself?

That shift in the stanza I quoted earlier, from the first person to the second, from an apparent self-absorption to a real concern with an other, is a very common pattern in Whitman's poetry. The first word of "Song of Myself," for instance, is *I*, but the last word is *you*, and the poem's opening stanza announces this larger pattern explicitly:

> I celebrate myself,
> And what I assume you shall assume,
> For every atom belonging to me as good belongs to you.
>   (1855, 25)

Looked at closely, both these stanzas reveal how anxious is the relationship they assert between *I* and *you*. The eternal present tense of "I celebrate myself" or "I know my own egotism" has to yield to time (the future tense of "shall assume") and chance (the conditional tense of "would fetch"). What looks at first like amplitude betrays its incompleteness; neither the celebrated self nor his own egotism is enough. As these tense changes indicate, the reader stands outside the circle Whitman is trying to draw. In "Song of Myself" *I* is everything, the whole cosmos, except *you*. Hundreds of other persons are referred to in the poem—prostitutes and presidents, runaway slaves and Texas Rangers—but they can be treated as parts of the self. *You*, on the other hand, though not strictly speaking "in" the poem at all, exists as a separate consciousness. Therefore *you* is the poem's only other character. *You* may in fact be the more important character. As the first line gives way to the second, it suddenly becomes unclear what the poem is about. Is its focus the self and the universe, or the self and the other, the poet and the reader? Which is the occasion for the poem—all that the *I* is or the one thing *I* isn't, that is, *you*?

As the first poem in the first edition of *Leaves of Grass*, "Song of Myself" is the place where Whitman premiered his identity as "Walt Whitman." Thinking of the poem as a performance might help with a problem that all the commentary on it has been unable to resolve. "Song of Myself" is one of the world's great long poems, but none of the many attempts to define its structure have been convincing. Unlike other long poems, as Quentin Anderson has pointed out, "Song of Myself" cannot tell a story without fatally compromising the claims to imperial selfhood that Whitman puts in for his *I*.[6] But if we conceive it generically as an epic poem, we will continue to expect a narrative structure of some kind. We are less likely to bring such expectations to a performance. "Song of Myself" is not a poem about "what happened"; instead, the poem itself, like any performance, is what is happening as it is being read. That is the when of the poem: the "this day and night" the reader spends with the poet, reading the poem (1855, 26). The dramatically charged space between Whitman and the reader is the where of the poem. The poem doesn't have a plot; it is a plot—it is organized around the reader, whose assumptions Whitman seeks to make over in his own image. Looking at "Song of Myself" for its structural design, in the way we can look for the structure of the *Iliad* or *Paradise Lost* or even *The Prelude*, will continue to frustrate critics because its design is essentially outward-looking, rhetorical, strategic. But once this distinction is grasped, we can realize that, like many other epic-length poems, this one announces its argument in its opening lines, as the poet advances out of the self to engage the reader's attention and to commit himself to a performance that will transform the reader. The hero is the poet as performer; the quest is to cross the gap between *I* and *you*. "What I assume you shall assume"—that transaction is the plot of "Song of Myself."

The distinction between story and strategy, between narrative and performative, has many implications. In this essay I can pursue only one: the way making the hero a performer subverts the poem's most grandiose claims, for Whitman, although the poem's creator as well as its hero, cannot finally determine the outcome of the performance plot. That depends on *you*, the readers "*up* there." In the poem *I* may seem to possess the power to roam freely through all of space and time, but in fact he has to keep coming back to his readers. He may try in the poem's second stanza to pose as a loafer "at my ease," but in fact he is working constantly—to fetch his readers to him. We in the audience can choose to attend to the performance on its own terms, and admire or censure, in any case be amazed by Whitman's egotism, his delight in himself, the sureness with which he exhibits that self to us. Whitman's cocky aplomb, his apparent adequacy to any occasion, even the occasion the poem creates of appearing naked before a crowd of strangers, is the absolute center of his performance. On the other hand, if we notice how dramatically and tirelessly he keeps thrusting himself at the audience, we might decide that deeper than his self-possession is an utter need for us, that the self he celebrates is not the pretext, the occasion for the performance, but instead exactly what the textual performance is trying to bring into existence. He explicitly gives his readers the power to *be* "Walt Whitman," but implicit in his preoccupation with holding their attention is the idea that it is actually the readers who have the power to *create* "Walt Whitman." At times Whitman can himself admit this dependency. At most times, of course, he asserts his godlike sovereignty: "I exist as I am, that is enough, / If no other in the world be aware I sit content, / ... One world is aware, and by far the largest to me, and that is myself" (1855, 44). Yet there is too much that such an assertion cannot account for, including Whitman's need to "exist as he is" in public. He comes closer to telling the truth about his rhetorical situation, his dependence on the awareness of others, when he says: "These are the thoughts of all men in all ages and lands, they are not original with me, / If they are not yours as much as mine they are nothing or next to nothing" (1855, 41). Since the "thoughts" revolve around the greatness of the self, it clearly follows that unless you celebrate that self too, the self itself is nothing or the next thing to it.

Without *you*, *I* am enough; without *you*, *I* am nothing: This contradiction is what makes Whitman's performative stance so hard to pin down. We can say that consistently he steps to the front of the poem to address his readers directly, but at those moments he speaks in many different tones of voice. He can be aggressive, taunting *your* assumptions: "Have you felt so proud to get at the meaning of poems?"; "Have you outstript the rest? Are you the President? / It is a trifle...." Or he can seriously ask for *your* opinions: "I wish I could translate the hints about the dead young men and women, / ... What do you think has become of the young and old men?" He can be nurturing: "Undrape .... you are not guilty to me, nor stale nor discarded." He can be threatening: "Encompass worlds but never try to encompass me, / I crowd your noisiest talk by looking toward you." He can be ingratiating: "This hour I tell things in confidence, / I might not tell everybody but I will tell you." It is also unclear how participatory the performance is. He regularly says that we must learn to celebrate our selves too: "All I mark as my own you shall offset it with your own." And he can define himself simply as our representative: "It is you talking just as much as myself .... I act as the tongue of you." But then there are moments when he asserts himself as our savior and master, and defines our selves merely as the extension of his will: "You there, impotent, loose in the knees, open your scarfed chops till I blow grit within you, / ... I do not ask who you are .... that is not important to me, / You can do nothing and be nothing but what I will infold you."[7] Is he up on stage to be the mirror of our selves, or are we in the audience to serve as the mirror of his self?

That question is one readers can best settle for themselves, and will perhaps answer differently at different points in the poem or on different readings of it. The related question I want to explore concerns the way Whitman changes the largest terms of the performance in "Song of Myself." At times he specifically depicts the rhetorical situation as a very public one. For example, the poem's peroration, the last eleven sections, begins with a dramatic signal that the performance is moving into its concluding act:

> ... A call in the midst of the crowd,
> My own voice, orotund sweeping and final.
>
> (1855, 73)

This trope identifies the poem's *I* as a kind of orator and the *you* as a crowd, a mass audience. In the poem's most striking figuration of the relationship between *I* and *you*, however, they meet privately, as two people, and the orotund call drops into a caressing whisper:

> Listener up there! Here you .... what have you to confide to me?
> Look in my face while I snuff the sidle of evening,
> Talk honestly, for no one else hears you, and I stay only a minute longer.
>
> (1855, 85)

Each of these passages is typical of a number of others. At one extreme the *you* of "Song of Myself" is the plural pronoun and refers to the American reading public, which Whitman addresses oratorically, democratically, impersonally. But if public oratory is one analogue for the kind of performance he is engaged in, seduction is another: At this extreme, *you* is the singular pronoun and refers to the solitary reader whom Whitman addresses personally, intimately, erotically. The date with *you* that he makes at the very end—"I stop some where waiting for you"—offers the prospect of a regenerate society, a new heaven and a new earth, and a chance at emotional fulfillment, a lover's rendezvous.

Watching Whitman perform in "Song of Myself" can be as disconcerting as watching Madonna on stage for the way it forces us to realize how much blurring there is between realms we might wish to keep distinct. There is probably always some sexual content in the public relationships between orators or entertainers and audiences, and some performative self-consciousness, some rhetoric, even in our moments of greatest intimacy. Certainly a major source of Whitman's power over our attention is his confessional breaching of the line most people draw between public and private, which is what he meant by saying "I remove the veil" (1855, 45), and which is what happens when he simultaneously seduces a crowd of strangers and puts on a show for a prospective lover. Where Whitman is large enough to contain contradictions, it would be a mistake for the critic to insist on resolving them too neatly. Betsy Erkkila rightly refers to this mixture of public and private as "Whitman's ever-shifting and shifty relationship with the *you* of the reader."[8] C. Carroll Hollis insightfully notes how Whitman's mode of address exploits an ambiguity peculiar to English as a language: that the same pronoun can be used as a singular or plural one: "The secret of Whitman's poetic maneuver here is that it [*you*] is *both* or *either*."[9] In "Song of Myself," *you* is both an individual and a crowd, and the performance is both a public and a private one. Yet if we keep the focus on Whitman's own imagination, we should be able to say which alternative predominates. In terms of the hopes, the ambitions, and desires that he invested in his poetry, was he writing mainly for a crowd of strangers or a lover?

What Whitman himself says about *you* can help us only up to a point. I've already quoted his favorite formulation; it was appended to the first *you* that appeared in this essay: "And would fetch you whoever you are flush with myself." "Whoever you are" is as sweeping as that call in the midst of the crowd, and is the only way to describe *you* consistent with his program to "accept nothing which all cannot have their counterpart of on the same terms" (1855, 48). For the most part, Whitman does define his readership this democratically. As part of his strategy in "Song of Myself," for example, he writes his own appreciative audience right into the poem itself. In what would become the forty-seventh of the poem's fifty-two sections, he pictures the way he and his "voice" and "words" have become part of the daily lives of the young mechanic, the woodman, the farm boy, fishermen and seamen, the hunter, the driver, the young and the old mothers, the girl and the wife (1855, 82). As an indication of whom he meant by *you*, although dominated by young men who work with their hands, this group of common men and women is consistent with such formulations as "you whoever you are" or "each man and each woman of you" (1855, 80).

The enthusiasm with which he imagines this audience responding to his poetry is a crucial aspect of the faith on which the whole vision of "Song of Myself" rests: that the greatness inherent in each man or woman's self will instantly recognize itself in Whitman's prophetic summons to greatness. Thus he was not bragging just on his own behalf, but on everybody's, when he wrote Emerson, in the public letter that he placed as an appendix to the second (1856) edition of *Leaves of Grass*:

> A few years, and the average call for my Poems is ten or twenty thousand copies—more, quite likely. Why should I hurry or compromise? In poems or speeches I say the word or two that has got to be said, adhere to the body, step with the countless common footsteps, and remind every man and woman of something. (1856, 346)

Numbers like these make *you* a very plural pronoun. An average yearly sale of over 20,000 copies would have made him the best-selling American poet of his time,[10] but these were appropriate numbers for him to be thinking in, given his democratic desire to speak the "word en masse" (1855, 47). And he was prepared to stake more than his faith in the common man and woman on such numbers. He was apparently prepared to let popularity be the measure of his greatness as a poet. The last line of the Preface to the first edition of *Leaves of Grass* asserts that "The proof of a poet is that his country absorbs him as affectionately as he has absorbed it" (1855, 24).

If Whitman believed in letting the majority rule this way on the issue of his own aesthetic achievement, his faith was sorely tested by the country's total failure to reciprocate his affection. Although he told Emerson (and every other reader of the 1856 *Leaves*) that the thousand copies of the 1855 edition had "readily sold" (1856, 346), he knew that his book's actual first year's sales had been closer to a dozen. Even most of the people to whom he had sent complimentary copies either ignored or condemned it. The truth about the book's reception is reflected in his decision to redefine the proof of a poet; much of the 1855 preface is recast in the 1856 *Leaves* as "Poem of Many in One," where Whitman now says: "The proof of a poet shall be sternly deferred till his country absorbs him as affectionately as he has absorbed it" (1856, 195).[11] There is a good deal of evidence to show that he wanted and expected *Leaves* to be quickly and widely popular, and that he was severely disappointed by its failure. Despite all such signs, however, I think we must wonder how he could have believed what he predicted about his own popularity.

It is not hard to understand why Whitman, who knew a lot about advertising, would want to mislead Emerson (and others) about how well his poetry was selling. But it is very hard to understand how he could have misled himself so spectacularly. Although in 1855, "Walt Whitman" was a new poet, Walter Whitman was no young man. As a thirty-six-year-old veteran of American journalism who had also published a temperance novel, he was an experienced man of letters. As someone who had edited newspapers well enough to increase their subscription lists, he was thoroughly acquainted with the prevailing appetites and expectations of the contemporary reading public. If the *you* of his poem is the average American reader of 1855, then "Song of Myself" was an almost complete assault on all *your* assumptions—about poetry, about religion, about the body, about life. Whitman knew this. It is what puts the tension in the tense changes whenever he shifts his focus from the self he can already celebrate or the physical world he can already devour with his omnivorous lines to the other, the reader, whom he *would* fetch or who *shall* share his assumptions. For all its celebratory mood, there are passages in the poem that indicate plainly, if obliquely, how deep was the gap between his and his potential readers' assumptions across which the performance had to carry; there is, for example, the passage about living "awhile with the animals" because "They do not make me sick discussing their duty to God, / ... not one is demented with the mania of owning things" (1855, 55, 56). How could Whitman have expected that Americans in 1855, who believed devoutly in owning things, and in God, would love his poetry?

Even more incredibly, to quote the question asked in the earliest English notice of Whitman's poems, "Is it possible that the most prudish nation in the world will adopt a poet whose indecencies stink in the nostrils?"[12] We need not agree with the judgments here—to me, there is nothing indecent about Whitman's poetry, and there may have been other nations as prudish as Victorian America. But this reviewer gets directly to the widest, deepest part of the gap between Whitman and his contemporary audience: his treatment of human sexuality. How could he have expected his culture to absorb his poems affectionately?

To me, this is the most perplexing of all the questions connected with Whitman's performance as an American poet. Perhaps he had temporarily lost touch with the reality of his literary and cultural situation; he might have been so wrapped up in the rapturous cosmic consciousness that the poem itself witnesses that he simply assumed his ecstasy would transport his audience with it into the new world—post-Christian, postcapitalist, postcultural—he claims for the self. The idea of a poet so absorbed in his own vision, however, would have to ignore Whitman's persistent, strategically shrewd preoccupation with *you*. Perhaps he was simply running the kind of bluff advertisers and politicians run all the time: declaring that the people love something in the hope of convincing at least some of them to do so. But that idea has to ignore his evident despair in the late 1850s at his poetry's unpopularity; if it's hard to believe how in 1855 he could have expected his poems to become popular, when we note his mood in 1857 and 1858, it becomes impossible to doubt that he had had such expectations. On the other hand, it is possible that there was a division in his own mind about his ambitions. Consciously, he may have needed to believe he was addressing a mass audience that would absorb him affectionately, while unconsciously knowing that only a few readers could be so receptive, but because he could not bring himself to admit that he was addressing such a "singular" *you*, he used the fiction of a democratic performance to disguise his desires even from himself.

I can put this complicated thought more simply by saying that I am talking about the problem of Whitman's homosexuality. I don't mean that it is a problem for us, although I have some anxiety about finding the right way to discuss it. I mean that it was a problem for Whitman. It might seem hypercritical to argue that the least inhibited nineteenth-century American writer—the prophet of the body and its polymorphous pleasures—was seriously repressed himself, but I think that the testimony of Whitman's whole life and work points to that conclusion. He could write much more evocatively, for example, about the beauty of the male physique than about the female, but could never bring himself to acknowledge that his attraction to men was sexual. Given the cultural circumstances of his era, it would have been extraordinarily difficult to discuss such desires publicly. Under no circumstances could he have said they were "homosexual," since that word did not even come into the English language until after his death. But the circumstances of his own temperament made it necessary for him to disguise his sexual preferences even from himself. He found a number of terms to describe "the love of comrades." His favorite, "adhesiveness," he took from phrenology, where the term stood for one's capacity to enter into high-minded, platonic friendships, especially, but not exclusively, with members of the same sex.[13]

Although it seems clear enough to most modern readers that with such terms Whitman is often expressing homoerotic desires, he himself insisted, as R. M. Bucke put it in the study of Whitman that Whitman silently coauthored, that comradeship was "an exalted friendship, a love into which sex does not enter as an element."[14] The most egregious public instance of this denial is the reply to John Addington Symonds, who had written to ask if Whitman's "conception of Comradeship" included any "semi-sexual emotions and actions": "the possibility of such construction," Whitman wrote back, "is terrible"; any such "inferences" are "disavow'd" as "damnable."[15] We can prove that out loud and in public, Whitman denied his homosexuality. I think that this pattern of denial extended into his psychic life as well: that even to himself he did not want to admit the truth about his sexuality.

This particular repression would, I suggest, provide the basis for an explanation of how Whitman used *you* in his poetry. He knew that what he wrote would profoundly offend or alienate most contemporary readers, but he had to believe it was democratically addressed to them all; in what he wrote he was seeking a specific audience—an audience of men who, like himself, had unacknowledged homoerotic longings—but could never be this specific, not even in his own mind. According to Walter J. Ong, a writer's audience is always a fiction,[16] but we can be specific about the kind of fiction Whitman's conflicted desires made necessary. The universal "you whoever you are" was his substitute for the more singular *you* he sought to communicate with. Whitman and this *you* meet surreptitiously in the figure of the one person mentioned in "Song of Myself" who comes closest to attaining the status of a character: the twenty-ninth bather he describes in section eleven, the woman who has unacknowledged desires for the naked young men bathing in the river.

Given the nature of repression, there is little direct evidence to support this idea of a singular *you* disguised as a plural one. An exception is the way Whitman began one of the three reviews he wrote and printed anonymously in 1855 to promote *Leaves of Grass*: "Very devilish to some, and very divine to some, will appear the poet of these new poems."[17] This is one of the few places where Whitman segregates his potential audience into different kinds of people, only "some" of whom, clearly, are ever likely to be interested in sharing his assumptions. There is also the remarkable avowal of his ambitions—again, as much private as public—that Whitman made in a footnote to the preface he wrote in 1876 for *Two Rivulets*. "I meant LEAVES OF GRASS," the passage begins, "to be the Poem of Identity, (of *Yours*, whoever you are, now reading these lines)." He goes on, in a passage worth quoting in full, to admit the emotional dissatisfaction out of which his poetry sprung. In this passage, as in "Out of the Cradle Endlessly Rocking," Whitman makes the connection between his poetry and "the cries of unsatisfied love" (1860, 276), though here without the screening fiction of the broken-hearted bird:

Something more may be added—for, while I am about it, I
would make a full confession. I also sent LEAVES OF GRASS to
arouse and set flowing in men's and women's hearts, young
and old, (my present and future readers,) endless streams of
living, pulsating love and friendship, directly from them to
myself, now and ever. To this terrible, irrepressible yearning,
(surely more or less down underneath in most human
souls,)—this never-satisfied appetite for sympathy, and this
boundless offering of sympathy—this universal democratic
comradeship—this old, eternal, yet ever-new interchange of
adhesiveness, so fitly emblematic of America—I have given
in that book, undisguisedly, declaredly, the openest
expression .... Poetic literature has long been the formal and
conventional tender of art and beauty merely, and of a
narrow, constipated, special amativeness. I say, the subtlest,
sweetest, surest tie between me and Him or Her, who, in the
pages of *Calamus* and other pieces realizes me—though we
never see each other, or though ages and ages hence—must,
in this way, be personal affection. And those—be they few, or
be they many—are at any rate *my readers*, in a sense that
belongs not, and can never belong, to better, prouder
poems.[18]

This is just about as full a confession as any writer is likely to give
us about the merely human longings that can provoke someone to
publish the self. Even here Whitman's characteristic defenses are on
display. He keeps trying to convert the unsettling realities of private
desire—terrible yearning, never-satisfied appetite—into the more
acceptable generalizations of public politics—emblematic of America,
democratic comradeship. And he is still trying to keep *you* from coming
too clearly into focus and so says "Him or Her"—although the idea of
"comradeship" has already excluded or at least marginalized "Her." But
what Whitman does so honestly in this passage is to debunk the myth of
creation that a poem like "Song of Myself" seeks to assert. There his
poetry is described as the overflowing of a self already full with the
cosmos, as when his own voice prods him to poetic speech: "Walt, you
understand enough ... why don't you let it out then?" (1855, 51). Here,
however, the figure he implicitly uses for himself is not the overflowing

fountain but the parched hollow, the empty vessel. The admission that literary performance is the quest for love, friendship, and sympathy helps us appreciate how literally we should be prepared to take a word like "affectionately" when Whitman uses it to define the relationship between a poet and his culture, or how literally Whitman means it when he says that he wants to "fetch" his reader "flush" with himself.

I hasten to add that it would be a mistake to take such conceptions too literally. We are still dealing with the make-believe world of performance, where fantasies remain fantasies even when they are "acted" out. In the actual world, I've said, Whitman could not even acknowledge having such desires, much less realize them. When he talks about having his desires "realized" by the reader of his poems, he is talking about an imaginative reality. In that world *I* and *you* can meet. This might seem to be a very frustrating, impersonal way to look for "personal affection," but in our age of the celebrity interview we have a vast amount of testimony from actors, actresses, and other performers about how being in the center of the stage and of an audience's attention can feel like being loved. What pushes performers onto the stage is often the need to get from a crowd of strangers what they cannot get from the people in their private lives. Seen this way, perhaps Whitman's tireless self-promotion—the reviews he wrote anonymously, the pictures he posed for, the news items he planted with editors, and so on[19]—seems less offensive.

We need to make a crucial distinction, though, between the imaginative performance a real performer engages in and the imaginative performance Whitman only *imagined*. Although he was deeply interested in all forms of performance, especially oratory and opera, and although at several points in his life he seems seriously to have considered attempting a career as an orator, especially in 1850–1 (before the first two editions of *Leaves of Grass*) and in 1857–8 (after those editions had failed so disastrously), in fact he lived out his fascination with performance the same way he lived out his sexual desires—vicariously. By writing about being in front of an audience, he made the relationship between *I* and *you* both more intimate (because reading is a private affair) and more impersonal (because, as he put it, "we never see each other"). Because the ambitions governing the performance were at once intimate and repressed, this indirect, mediated relationship with an other suited him much better than a more literal kind of public appearance could have done.[20]

Walter Whitman's transformation in the mid-1850s into the "Walt Whitman" who springs forth from the pages of *Leaves of Grass* is one of the great aesthetic miracles in American literary history. It will never be possible to explain such a transformation completely. But we can begin to account for the particular way "Song of Myself" addresses its audience with the idea that Whitman transferred his erotic longings to the realm of literary performance, where he could express them by disguising the *you* he wanted to court as the common reader of his time. This would help explain, for instance, how he could write what he had to know would be "devilish" to most readers in 1855 while nonetheless believing that it would be "affectionately absorbed" by them. Real popularity would have served Whitman in many ways, but the mere fiction that he was writing to be popular was equally valuable. That it was the fiction of being popular he needed would explain why, unlike Ralph Waldo Emerson or Mark Twain (to cite two other writers equally preoccupied with performing), Whitman would not make the compromises with or concessions to his audience's values that would have made real popularity at all possible.

I think this idea can also help us appreciate the performative rhythms of "Song of Myself." The way Whitman commingles public with private, politics with sexuality, the way *you* at times refers to a crowd of listeners and at others to a solitary reader, the way the poet's tone of voice runs the gamut from the stridency of the orator to the tenderness of the suitor—all of this is consistent with the notion of Whitman's divided rhetorical ambitions and the need to keep the division hidden from himself. "Song of Myself" as a little "r" romantic quest for love has to appear in the guise of a big "R" Romantic cultural manifesto. Whitman can advance toward intimacy with *you* as a singular reader only so far before needing to pull back to the psychically safer terms of a public relationship with *you* as his democratic audience.

David Leverenz is one of the few commentators to talk about what it feels like to be *you*, to articulate the emotional experience of reading "Song of Myself." For him that experience is similarly ambivalent: "I like [Whitman's] bold brag about my hidden strength of self, even when he claims to be my tongue. I welcome his call to 'fetch' me 'flush with myself,' so long as 'myself' includes me as well as him, and so long as his 'I' evokes a vaguely arrogant spirit rather than a specifically desiring body. My resistance leaps into consciousness when he gets too physical with me."[21] I know what he means—there are moments when Whitman crowds me too closely—but on the whole, in my reading of it, "Song of Myself" is well served by the balance it maintains between oratory and seduction. When Whitman personalizes *you* as a singular reader we can feel the intensity of his concern with us, but whenever this begins to feel threatening, the poem allows us to step back into the safety of being part of a crowd. I think this balance is one reason why, with most readers, "Song of Myself" is his most successful performance poem. The same needs, however, that pushed Whitman up onto the stage he created in that poem led him to try to get still closer to the reader. The poem that immediately follows "Song of Myself" in the 1855 *Leaves*, for example, begins:

> Come closer to me,
> Push close my lovers and take the best I possess,
> Yield closer and closer and give me the best you possess.
> This is unfinished business with me .... how is it with you?
> I was chilled with the cold types and cylinder and wet paper between us.
> I pass so poorly with paper and types .... I must pass with the contact
>   of bodies and souls.

> (1855, 87)

By thus struggling to erase the distance between *I* and *you* that the written word made possible, Whitman is making demands of the reading process and on the reader that most people find impossible to understand, much less accept. At the center of the most significant new poem in the 1856 *Leaves of Grass* is again an encounter between *I* and *you*, but now the relationship is carried to an extreme beyond which not even Whitman could subsequently go.

The poem, eventually titled "Crossing Brooklyn Ferry," was called "Sun-Down Poem" in 1856. The encounter it dramatizes occurs between Whitman and the readers or reader (I'll discuss the difference) of the future, "of a generation, or ever so many generations hence" (1856, 212). That Whitman moves his audience into the future is an oblique indication of how badly the 1855 *Leaves* had done with the contemporary reading public. Once Whitman evokes this future audience, he writes about it in the present tense while writing about himself in the past: "Just as you stand and lean on the rail ... I stood"

(1856, 213). The grammatical gimmick displays the same lovely insouciance as many of Whitman's most nonchalant refusals to worry about death: Even when he exists only in the past tense, he's still very much alive to his readers. This is Whitman's characteristic redefinition of the trope of poetic immortality: It is not in art per se that he can transcend death, but in art as the means by which he reaches an audience that is always being generationally renewed; he doesn't live in the poem, but in the minds of that audience. Yet the poem also suggests that Whitman had another reason for projecting his readers into the future, and that there was something besides immortality that he wanted from an audience.

If Whitman's deepest desire was for eternal fame, then the best referent for *you* in a phrase like "you who peruse me" (1856, 220) would naturally be plural: the largest possible number of readers. This is what *you* stands for at the beginning: "Crowds of men and women" on the ferry with Whitman become "you men and women" of the future, who will ride the ferry as he did (1856, 211, 212). In the course of the poem, though, both *I* and *you* advance out of these crowds toward each other— "Closer yet I approach you" (1856, 118)—until we get to a line like "It is not you alone, nor I alone" (1856, 218), which, although written in the negative, clearly implies two people, an *I* and a *you*. The poem's climax is the mystical communion of these two in the eternal present tense of the immediate reading of the poem; all falls away except *I* and *you*, who become a seamless *we*:

> Now I am curious what sight can ever be more stately and admirable to me
>   than my mast-hemm'd Manhatta,
> My river and sun-set, and my scallop-edged waves of flood tide,
> The sea-gulls oscillating their bodies, the hay-boat in the twilight,
>   the belated lighter;
> Curious what Gods can exceed these that clasp me by the hand, and with voices
>   I love call me promptly and loudly by my nighest name as I approach,
> Curious what is more subtle than this which ties me to the woman or man
>   that looks in my face,
> Which fuses me into you now, and pours my meaning into you.
>
> We understand, then, do we not?
> What I promised without mentioning it, have you not accepted?

What the study could not teach—what the preaching could not accomplish
  is accomplished, is it not?
What the push of reading could not start is started by me personally, is it not?
                              (1856, 218–19)

    Such absolute communion, such transcendence of all signs of
otherness—even the words and the reading through which the meeting
takes place—is the extreme beyond which Whitman could not go in his
attempt to express his ideal relationship with his reader. But although he
couldn't go beyond it, he arrived at the same extreme again in the well-
known assertion he makes in "*So Long!*," the poem he put last in the
third, 1860, edition of *Leaves of Grass*; "*So Long!*," which he used to close
the performance in every subsequent edition of *Leaves*, expresses the
relationship in still more intimate terms:

My songs cease—I abandon them,
From behind the screen where I hid, I advance personally.

This is no book,
Who touches this, touches a man,
(Is it night? Are we here alone?)
It is I you hold, and who holds you,
I spring from the pages into your arms—decease calls me forth.

O how your fingers drowse me!
Your breath falls around me like dew—your pulse lulls the tympans
  of my ears,
I feel immerged from head to foot.
Delicious—enough.
                              (1860, 455)

    While I think most readers are intrigued by these two passages, I
expect they probably decline to play the part of imaginary lover that
Whitman writes for them in both. They remain readers holding a book,
mystified and—if they think about it seriously—uncomfortable with the
idea of suddenly finding a strange man in their arms. But I think these
passages reveal how Whitman sought love or, more accurately, erotic
satisfaction in the realm of art, where his private imaginings became

public performances of these personal encounters. And although they indicate this desire with almost embarrassing nakedness, I think these passages also confirm what I've been saying about his need to disguise as well as sublimate that quest. For example, they both describe encounters in the dark: What "*So Long!*" seems to require as a precondition for meeting the reader, that it is "night," "Crossing Brooklyn Ferry" helps us appreciate. Though thematically a point of the poem is that all time, time present and time future, is one, it nonetheless carefully tracks the passage of the time between sundown (when the poem begins) and night (when *we* come together). Exactly as *I* and *you* move closer to that moment when *I* am fused into *you*, so does the light disappear; the scene becomes "dimmer and dimmer" (1856, 215), until all that can be seen are "the fires from the foundry chimneys burning high and glaringly into the night" (1856, 215).

If the darkness is essential to hide the very encounter that Whitman is about to express, it is also appropriately what makes it possible to see the fires flaming forth, for throughout Whitman's early poetry, outflaming fires are a favorite image of the desires that he admits are hard to acknowledge. As he puts it in the first poem of the 1860 *Leaves*, talking specifically about "the ideal of manly love": "I will therefore let flame from me the burning fires that were threatening to consume me, / I will lift what has too long kept down those smouldering fires" (1860, 11). What in fact forms the immediate bond between the *I* and *you* who merge on the ferry in the "wild red and yellow light" of the flames (1856, 215) are the passions and feelings that Whitman calls "the dark patches" that are usually hidden in shame: "guile, anger, lust, hot wishes I dared not speak" (1856, 217). By confessing these desires without guilt in himself and identifying them in his reader without judgment, Whitman makes these "dark patches" the common ground on which he and his reader meet. They are not exactly unrepressed, however; they remain in wordlessness, the poetic equivalent of impenetrable darkness. The hot wishes remain unspoken, and what the reader "accepts" remains "unmentioned."

The other and most remarkable "screen" to the encounter between *I* and *you* in both these passages is death. "Decease calls me forth," Whitman writes in "*So Long!*" It is not a living man who steps in front of his songs to hold and be held by the reader, but a dead one—which makes the embrace at once more mystical and considerably less erotic.

The passage both revels in bodily sensuality—arms, fingers, breath, pulse, delicious—and *dis*embodies the poetic self. Even at this extreme of intimacy, alone in the dark with *you*, Whitman is talking about something that can only happen imaginatively, not physically. This is equally true about the union with the reader he stages in "Crossing Brooklyn Ferry." "I project myself," he notes at the start (1856, 215), establishing what the poem's distribution of verb tenses also underlines: He draws nearer to the reader only as a kind of holy spirit, a self that no longer possesses the body in which it stood by the ferry's rail. Again the diction is physical—fuse into, pour into, push—but the encounter is strictly metaphysical.

If we look again at "Song of Myself," we see the same pattern even there. As I said, throughout the poem he is continually moving closer to and farther from the reader; at the end he stops and makes a date—"I stop some where waiting for you"—but again, only after he has died and presided over his own bodily dissolution. The most explicit instance of this pattern occurs in the poem he put at the end of the "Calamus" sequence, where in the first two lines Whitman goes from being "Full of life" to dead, and in the next two the reader gets pushed into the distant future—at least "a century hence." *I* and *you* actually become lovers in this poem, but only in the poem—because *I* "seeking you" am dead, and *you* are "you, yet unborn":

> When you read these, I, that was visible, am become invisible;
> Now it is you, compact, visible, realizing my poems, seeking me,
> Fancying how happy you were, if I could be with you, and become your lover;
> Be it as if I were with you. Be not too certain but I am now with you.
>
> (1860, 378)

"*As if*"—these are the two words that govern Whitman's relationship with his reader. One of Whitman's most impressive achievements as the poet of common reality is his ability to dispense almost entirely with metaphor. This metaphor, however, was the one that as a performer he could not do without. "As if" *I* and *you* were alone together is what enables him simultaneously to express and repress the longings that governed the dynamics of his literary performance.

The "Calamus" sequence is the most significant addition to *Leaves of Grass* in the 1860 edition. I don't have space to discuss the sequence in any detail, but I should mention the way it constitutes the last movement in Whitman's attempt to redefine the nature of poetic performance. (As Ezra Greenspan has noted, in most of the poems he wrote after 1860 Whitman is in "retreat from this reader-in-the-text strategy."[22]) Like "Song of Myself" and "Crossing Brooklyn Ferry," the "Calamus" poems as a group are very illocutionary, very much organized as a performance for a *you* the poems keep coming back to. By writing and publishing these poems, Whitman is moving in the direction of his private desires—"To tell the secret of my nights and days" (1860, 342)—and away from the values or assumptions he could expect his larger culture to share. He still cannot admit this into consciousness, and so he treats "the need of comrades" (1860, 342) and the secret love of strangers (1860, 362) as a political rather than a sexual theme: "The dependence of Liberty shall be lovers, / The continuance of Equality shall be comrades" (1860, 351). As he put it in prose in 1876, "the special meaning of the *Calamus* cluster ... mainly resides in its political sig-nificance."[23] But of all Whitman's poems, these come closest to appealing directly to a singular *you*.

Even here he cannot escape his mixed emotions, and as Betsy Erkkila has noted, throughout the sequence *you* refers to everything from "America and democracy" to "an exclusive group" to "an intimate lover."[24] "Whoever You Are Holding Me Now in Hand," the third poem in the sequence, begins with Whitman's familiar assertion of equal opportunity, a universal *you*, but then quickly sets up a specific entrance requirement to the rest of the poems: "Who is he that would become my follower? / Who would sign himself a candidate for my affections? Are you he?" (1860, 345). The forty-five poems in "Calamus" move back and forth from the front of the stage where Whitman can address the reader directly, and variously define that reader in general and in very particular terms, but I think the tendency of the whole sequence is made manifest in the forty-first poem, which leaves the mass audience behind: "Among the men and women, the multitude, I perceive one picking me out by secret and divine signs, / ... Some are baffled—But that one is not—that one knows me" (1860, 376). This passage brings the tension between his private needs and the public performance in which he sought to satisfy them right up to the surface of the poetry. Either the love of comrades is what knits the multitude together, or it is what distinguishes the few from that multitude, but it cannot be both.

To fix this squarely on the tension that I've suggested inheres in the performance itself: Either he is telling "the thoughts of all men in all ages and lands," as he put it in "Song of Myself" (1855, 41), or he is making "secret and divine signs" that only one other will know how to interpret. Of course, in terms of what I've tried to say about the psychic dynamic of Whitman's performance, it was both—in the sense that he was writing for a restricted *you* but had to see it himself as a universal one. In the first three editions of *Leaves*, between 1855 and 1860, he moved steadily further from defining the relationship between *I* and *you* as the democratic prophet speaking oratorically to the crowd and closer to enacting it as a private affair, as two lovers alone in the dark. But even as he came closer to identifying *you* this specifically, and closer to an explicit account of what "fetch you flush with myself" might mean, he projected *you* into the future. When he makes that strange leap in "*So Long!*"—"I spring from these pages into your arms"—he is, as the very last line of *Leaves of Grass* continued to say from 1860 until the final edition of 1892, "as one disembodied, triumphant, dead." In terms of what I'm saying about how he imagined the encounter with his reader, the first of those three adjectives may be the most important. We can say that seeking *you* through poetry is one means to triumph over death. We can also say, however, that seeking *you* through poetry was not unlike death: As "Walt Whitman" he is a "disembodied" lover.

NOTES

1. *Walt Whitman's Leaves of Grass: The First (1855) Edition*, ed. Malcolm Cowley (New York: Viking, 1959), p. 74. Subsequent references to Whitman's poetry will be cited in parentheses in text. Because one of my concerns is to trace changes in Whitman's performance as he enacted them during the 1850s, and not with his subsequent revisions, I quote in every case from the earliest version of a poem. All references to the first edition of *Leaves of Grass* will be to Cowley's widely available reprinting of it, cited as 1855, followed by the page number. All references to the second edition will be to the original issue: *Leaves of Grass* (Brooklyn, 1856), cited as 1856, followed by the page number. All references to the third edition will be to Roy Harvey Pearce's modern facsimile reprinting *Leaves of Grass, By Walt Whitman:*

Facsimile Edition of the 1860 Text, ed. Pearce (Ithaca, N.Y.: Cornell University Press, 1961)—cited as 1860, followed by the page number.

2. Hollis, *Language and Style in Leaves of Grass* (Baton Rouge: Louisiana State University Press, 1983), p. 98.

3. See especially the chapter called "Speech Acts" (*Language and Style*, pp. 65–123). "Illocutionary" is John Searle's term.

4. *Walt Whitman and the American Reader* (Cambridge: Cambridge University Press, 1960), p. 196. Hollis and Greenspan have done the most interesting recent work on the role of the reader in Whitman's poetry; my analysis of that topic, I think, complements theirs.

5. *Walt Whitman: Notebooks and Unpublished Prose Manuscripts*, ed. Edward F. Grier, 6 vols., I: *Family Notebooks and Autobiography: Brooklyn and New York* (New York: New York University Press, 1984), p. 202.

6. "Whitman's New Man" in *Walt Whitman: Walt Whitman's Autograph Revision of the Analysis of Leaves of Grass (For Dr. R. M. Bucke's Walt Whitman)*, text notes by Stephen Railton (New York: New York University Press, 1974), pp. 24–5.

7. Four dots (....) are Whitman's markers in the 1855 text; three dots indicate my ellipses. The quotations in this paragraph are, respectively, from pages 26, 45, 30, 51, 43, 43, 82, and 70.

8. Erkkila, *Whitman: The Political Poet* (New York: Oxford University Press, 1989), p. 182; she goes on to survey the various antecedents for *you* that can be found in the "Calamus" poems.

9. Hollis, *Language and Style*, p. 94.

10. During Whitman's career, the best-selling American poet was Longfellow. According to William Charvat, Longfellow's most popular book of verse—*Hiawatha*, also published in 1855—sold just over 50,000 copies in thirteen years (see Charvat, *The Profession of Authorship in America, 1800–1870*, ed. Matthew J. Bruccoli [n.p.: Ohio State University Press, 1968], p. 140).

11. In 1882 Whitman reprinted the 1855 preface in *Specimen Days and Collect*; one of the revisions he made at that time was to leave out the "proof of a poet" idea entirely (see *Walt Whitman: Leaves of Grass, Comprehensive Reader's Edition*, ed. Harold W. Blodgett and Sculley Bradley [New York: New York University Press, 1965], p. 729).

12. From the (London) *Critic*, April 1, 1856; quoted in *Walt Whitman: The Critical Heritage*, ed. Milton Hindus (New York: Barnes & Noble, 1971), p. 56.

13. See Michael Lynch, "'Here Is Adhesiveness': From Friendship to Homosexuality," *Victorian Studies* 29 (1985):67–96.

14. Bucke, *Walt Whitman*, p. 86.

15. Justin Kaplan does a good job telling the story of this exchange, and prints both Symonds's and Whitman's letters, in his biography: *Walt Whitman: A Life* (Toronto: Bantam Books, 1982), pp. 45–8.

16. Ong, "The Writer's Audience Is Always a Fiction," *PMLA* 90 (1975):9–21.

17. From the *Brooklyn Daily Times*; reprinted in *Walt Whitman: The Critical Heritage*, p. 45.

18. *Leaves of Grass, Comprehensive Reader's Edition*, p. 751.

19. Edward F. Grier, for example, lists almost fifty items of what he refers to as Whitman's "self-advertisements" in his edition of Whitman's notebooks and adds that "a close reading of the gossip columns of newspapers in New York, Washington, Philadelphia, and Camden ... would probably turn up a large number of items [Whitman] planted": *Walt Whitman: Notebooks and Unpublished Prose Manuscripts*, I, p. 333.

20. Hollis, on the other hand, argues that even as a poet, Whitman was an "orator manqué," who would have preferred to address his culture orally but who was temperamentally unsuited to such a performance, and so turned to writing by default (see *Language and Style in Leaves of Grass*, pp. 79ff. and 227).

21. Leverenz, *Manhood and the American Renaissance* (Ithaca, N.Y.: Cornell University Press, 1989), p. 31.

22. Greenspan, *Walt Whitman and the American Reader*, p. 221. For good accounts of the way Whitman's poetry changed after 1860, see the entire last chapter of Greenspan's book. See also Hollis, *Language and Style in Leaves of Grass*, passim.

23. Whitman, "Preface 1876," in *Comprehensive Reader's Edition*, p. 751.

24. Erkkila, *Whitman: The Political Poet*, pp. 182–3.

Chronology

1816	Walter Whitman, Sr. and Louisa Van Velsor marry.
1819	May 31st, Walter Whitman, Jr. born to Louisa Van Velsor and Walter Whitman, Sr. at West Hills near Huntington Station, NY, the second born of eight children, descended from the earliest Dutch and English inhabitants of Long Island.
1823	Whitman family moves to Brooklyn where he attends public school until 1830.
1829	As a young boy of 10, Whitman hears radical Quaker orator, Elias Hicks speak and identifies with his thoughts on "sanctity of self."
1830-31	Whitman works as an office boy.
1834	Whitman's family moves back to Long Island. Whitman, then 15, stays in New York City and works at *The Mirror* frequenting the theatre and traveling the ferry line daily.
1831-35	Learns printing trade as an apprentice on Democratic newspaper *Patriot* and then the *Star* and then as a printer until the great New York City fire on August 12.
1835	Great New York City Fire, August 12, devastates the printing industry forcing Whitman to move back to Long Island with his family.

1836-38	Schoolteacher in various Long Island towns including East Norwich, Hempstead, Babylon, Long Swamp, Smithtown.
1838-39	Founds and edits *Long-Islander* at Huntington, then works on Jamaica *Democrat*. Composes early poems including "Sun-Down papers from the Desk of a Schoolmaster" while teaching at Little Bay Side School near Jamaica. Begins sketches.
1840-41	Campaigns for election of Martin Van Buren, then returns to teaching at Trimming Square, Woodbury, Dix Hills, and Whitestone.
1841	In May, returns to New York City, remains active in Democratic party contributing to *Democratic Review*; works as printer for *New World*.
1842-1845	Edits daily newspapers, *The New York Aurora* and the *Evening Tattler* for several months. Writes his only novel, *Franklin Evans*, which will become the best selling work of his life.
1845-1848	Works in Brooklyn again for the *Star* (Sept. 1845-March, 1846) and the *Daily Eagle* (March, 1846-Jan., 1848).
1848	February, travels to New Orleans via railroad, stagecoach, and steamboat; employed on *New Orleans Crescent* as editor.
1848-1849	Joins "Free Soil" movement and edits *Brooklyn Freeman*.
1849-1854	Returns to his family in Long Island; his notebooks from 1853-1854 are basis for *Leaves of Grass*.
1855	Early June, independently publishes first edition of *Leaves of Grass*, a collection of twelve untitled poems including what later is titled "Song of Myself" and "The Sleepers." Sadness at death of father on July 11 is followed by elation at receiving Ralph Waldo Emerson's letter praising *Leaves of Grass* and Whitman. Public reception to work is lukewarm.
1856	Second edition of *Leaves of Grass*, including original twelve and new poem, eventually entitled "Crossing

Brooklyn Ferry." Emerson's letter of praise and Whitman's reply to it are also included in this volume. Henry David Thoreau and Bronson Alcott visit Whitman in Brooklyn.

1857-1859   Editor, *Brooklyn Times*, where he writes numerous editorials on slavery and continues writing poetry. Suffers depression from late 1858-1859 based on a speculated failed homoerotic relationship.

1860   Thayer and Eldridge in Boston publish third edition of *Leaves of Grass*, featuring "Calamus" poems and poem to be entitled "Out of the Cradle Endlessly Rocking" and "As I Ebb'd with the Ocean of Life." While proofing volume in Boston, Whitman visits Emerson.

1861-62   April 12, Civil War begins with battle at Fort Sumter. Whitman returns to journalism, spends time visiting sick and war-weary at New York Hospital.

1862   In December, searches for wounded brother George at the Virginia battlefield, Fredericksburg, and stays in camp for several weeks.

1863-1864   Stays in Washington, D.C., during period referred to as "Wound Dresser" years, visiting war-wounded at area hospitals and working at Paymaster's Office. In mid-June Whitman returns to Brooklyn due to ill health.

1865   In January, appointed as clerk at Department of the Interior only to be dismissed in June because of scandal surrounding third edition of *Leaves of Grass*. Attends Lincoln's second inauguration on March 4th and mourns his death on April 14th by composing "When Lilacs Last in Dooryard Bloom'd" during the summer. Elegy published late October in *Drum-Taps* and *Sequel*. Year ends on a happy note with release of brother George from a Confederate prison. Meets Peter Doyle, aged 18.

1866   Novel about Whitman, written by William D. O'Connor entitled *Good Grey Poet* published by Bunce & Harrington, New York City.

1867	Fourth edition of *Leaves of Grass* is published; *Democracy* (part of later *Democratic Vistas)* is published in December *Galaxy*.
1868	Whitman elated at publication of first biography by John Burroughs' entitled *Notes on Walt Whitman as Poet and Person*.
1870	Fifth edition of *Leaves of Grass; Democratic Vistas*. Whitman enters another period of depression for personal reasons.
1873	Paralytic stroke in January followed by death of his mother in May; moves to Camden to live with brother George in June to recuperate. Suffers depression from physical disabilities and distancing from Peter Doyle.
1876	Sixth edition of *Leaves of Grass*, including "Two Rivulets" is published. Whitman's financial condition is dire and is largely supported by overseas friends.
1879-80	Travels to American West and Canada delivering first public lectures on Abraham Lincoln.
1881	Emerson and Whitman meet in Concord, Massachusetts for final time. Works on seventh edition of *Leaves of Grass*.
1882	*Leaves of Grass*, seventh edition is published and immediately is banned in Boston. Whitman is visited by Oscar Wilde in Camden. *Specimen Days* is published.
1883	Second biography, *Walt Whitman*, published by Dr. R.M. Bucke with Whitman's assistance.
1884	Buys first and only house on Mickle Street in Camden, New Jersey.
1887	Whitman the subject of many works of art including a sculpture by Sidney Morse, and paintings by Herbert Gilchrist, J.W. Alexander and Thomas Eakins.
1888	Severe paralytic stroke.
1898	Published eighth edition of *Leaves of Grass* in honor of his 70th birthday with assistance of Horace Traubel, includes Prefatory Letter to Readers and "Sands at

Seventy." Friends host a birthday dinner, the proceedings of which were published as *Camden's Compliments.*

1891   *Good-Bye My Fancy* and ninth edition, known as the "deathbed edition," of *Leaves of Grass* published.

1892   Death of Whitman, March 26 in Camden; buried in Harleigh Cemetery, Camden, New Jersey.

Works by Walt Whitman

Franklin Evans or The Inebriate. (1842)
Leaves of Grass, nine editions. (1855-1892)
Democratic Vistas. (1870)
Specimen Days and Collect. (1882)
Good By My Fancy. (1891)

Works about Walt Whitman

Allen, Gay Wilson. *The New Walt Whitman Handbook*. New York: Hendricks House, 1962.

———. *The Solitary Singer: A Critical Biography of Walt Whitman*. New York: New York University Press, 1967 (first pub. 1955).

Aspiz, Harold. "The Body Politic in *Democratic Vistas*." *Walt Whitman: The Centennial Essays*, ed. by Ed Folsom. Iowa City: University of Iowa Press, 1994.

———. *Walt Whitman and the Body Beautiful*. Urbana: University of Illinois Press, 1980.

Asselineau, Roger. *The Evolution of Walt Whitman*. 2 vols. Cambridge: Harvard University Press, 1960-62.

Bloom, Harold, ed. *Walt Whitman, Bloom's Major Poets*. Philadelphia: Chelsea House Publishers, 1999.

———. *Walt Whitman*. New York: Chelsea House, 1985.

Callow, Philip. From Noon to Starry Night: A Life of Walt Whitman. Chicago: I.R. Dee, 1992.

Cather, Willa. "['sometimes sublime, sometimes ridiculous']." *Critical Essays on Walt Whitman*, ed. by James Woodress. Boston: G.K. Hall, 1983.

Chari, V. K. "Whitman and Indian Thought." *Western Humanities Review*, 13 (1959), 291-302.

Chase, Richard. *Walt Whitman Reconsidered*. New York: William Sloane Associates, Inc., 1955.

Cmiel, Kenneth. *Democratic Eloquence: The Fighter over Popular Speech in Nineteenth-Century America*. New York: Morrow, 1990.

Conway, Moncure D. Review of *Leaves of Grass*. *Walt Whitman: The Contemporary Reviews*, ed. by Kenneth M. Price. Cambridge: Cambridge University Press, 1996.

Cowley, Malcolm. "Editor's Introduction." *Walt Whitman's* Leaves of Grass: *The First (1855) Edition.* New York: The Viking Press, 1959.

Dana, Charles A. "New Publications: *Leaves of Grass.*" *Walt Whitman: The Contemporary Reviews,* ed. by Kenneth M. Price. Cambridge: Cambridge University Press, 1996.

Donoghue, Denis. "Walt Whitman." *American Literature to 1900,* ed. by Marcus Cunliffe. New York: Peter Bedrick Books, 1987.

Dressman, Michael Rowan. "Walt Whitman's Plans for the Perfect Dictionary." *Studies in the American Renaissance,* ed. Joel Myerson. Boston: Twayne, 1979.

Emerson, Ralph Waldo. *Essays: First and Second Series.* New York: Vintage Books, 1990.

Erkkila, Betsy and Jay Grossman, eds. *Breaking Bounds: Walt Whitman and American Cultural Studies.* New York: Oxford University Press, 1996.

Erkkila, Betsy. "Whitman and the Homosexual Republic." *Walt Whitman: The Centennial Essays,* ed. by Ed Folsom. Iowa City: University of Iowa Press, 1994.

———. *Whitman the Political Poet.* New York: Oxford University Press, 1989.

Fanner, Robert D. *Walt Whitman and Opera.* Philadelphia: University of Pennsylvania Press, 1951.

Feidelson, Charles, Jr. *Symbolism and American Literature.* Chicago: University of Chicago Press, 1953.

Fern, Fanny. "Fresh Fern Leaves: Leaves of Grass." *Walt Whitman: The Contemporary Reviews,* ed. by Kenneth M. Price. Cambridge: Cambridge University Press, 1996.

Folsom, Ed., ed. *Walt Whitman Quarterly Review.* Iowa City: University of Iowa Press.

———, ed. *Walt Whitman: The Centennial Essays.* Iowa City: University of Iowa Press, 1994.

Gilchrist, Anne. "An Englishwoman's Estimate of Walt Whitman." *Critical Essays on Walt Whitman,* ed. by James Woodress. Boston: G.K. Hall, 1983.

Golden, Arthur. "The Obfuscations of Rhetoric: Whitman and the Visionary Experience." In *Walt Whitman: The Centennial Essays,* ed. by Ed Folsom. Iowa City: University of Iowa Press, 1994.

Greenspan, Ezra, ed. *The Cambridge Companion to Walt Whitman.* Cambridge: Cambridge University Press, 1995.

Griswold, Rufus W. Review of *Leaves of Grass. Walt Whitman: The Contemporary Reviews,* ed. by Kenneth M. Price. Cambridge: Cambridge University Press, 1996.

Hale, Edward Everett. Review of *Leaves of Grass. Walt Whitman: The Contemporary Reviews*, ed. by Kenneth M. Price. Cambridge: Cambridge University Press, 1996.

Hindus, Milton, ed. *Walt Whitman: The Critical Heritage*. London: Routledge, 1971.

Hollis, C. Carroll. *Language and Style in* Leaves of Grass. Baton Rouge: Louisiana State University Press, 1963.

Howells, William Dean. "[A Young Novelist Fails to Appreciate *Drum-Taps*]." In *Critical Essays on Walt Whitman*, ed. by James Woodress. Boston: G.K. Hall, 1983.

Hyde, Lewis. *The Gift: Imagination and the Erotic Life of Property*. New York: Vintage Books, 1983.

James, C.L.R. "Whitman and Melville." *The C.L.R. James Reader*, ed. by Anna Grimshaw. Cambridge, Mass.: Blackwell, 1992.

James, Henry. "[Another Fledgling Novelist Disparages *Drum-Taps*]." *Critical Essays on Walt Whitman*, ed. by James Woodress. Boston: G.K. Hall, 1983.

James, William. "The Religion of Healthy-Mindedness." *Critical Essays on Walt Whitman*, ed. by James Woodress. Boston: G.K. Hall, 1983.

Jarrell, Randall. "Some Lines from Whitman." *No Other Book: Selected Essays*. New York: HarperCollins, 1999.

Kaplan, Justin. *Walt Whitman: A Life*. New York: Simon and Schuster, 1980.

Killingsworth, M. Jimmie. *Whitman's Poetry of the Body: Sexuality, Politics, and the Text*. Chapel Hill: University of North Carolina Press, 1989.

Krieg, Joann, ed. *Walt Whitman: Here and Now*. Westport, Conn.: Greenwood Press, 1985.

Leipold, L. Edmond. *Famous American Poets*. Minneapolis: Denison, 1969.

Leverenz, David. *Manhood and the American Renaissance*. Ithaca: Cornell University Press, 1989.

Lewis, R.W.B. *The American Adam: Innocence, Tragedy and Tradition in the Nineteenth Century*. Chicago: University of Chicago Press, 1955.

Loving, Jerome. "Emerson, Whitman, and the Paradox of Self-Reliance." *Critical Essays on Walt Whitman*, ed. by James Woodress. Boston: G.K. Hall, 1983.

Lawrence, D.H. "Whitman." *Critical Essays on Walt Whitman*, ed. by James Woodress. Boston: G.K. Hall, 1983.

Miller, James E., Jr. *A Critical Guide to* Leaves of Grass. Chicago: The University of Chicago Press, 1957.

————. "The Care and Feeding of American Long Poems: The American Epic from Barlow to Berryman." *Critical Essays on Walt Whitman*, ed. by James Woodress. Boston: G.K. Hall, 1983.

Myerson, Joel. *Walt Whitman: A Descriptive Bibliography*. Pittsburgh: University of Pittsburgh Press, 1993.

Nathanson, Tenney. *Whitman's Presence: Body, Voice, and Writing in* Leaves of Grass. New York: New York University Press, 1992.

Norton, Charles Eliot. "Whitman's *Leaves of Grass*." *Walt Whitman: The Contemporary Reviews*, ed. by Kenneth M. Price. Cambridge: Cambridge University Press, 1996.

O'Connor, William Douglas. "The Good Gray Poet: A Vindication." *Critical Essays on Walt Whitman*, ed. by James Woodress. Boston: G.K. Hall, 1983.

Orvell, Miles. *The Real Thing: Imitation and Authenticity in American Culture, 1880-1940*. Chapel Hill: University of North Carolina Press, 1989.

Pearce, Roy Harvey. *The Continuity of America Poetry*. Princeton: Princeton University Press, 1961.

Perry, Bliss. *Walt Whitman: His Life and Work*. Boston: Houghton, 1906.

Pollak, Vivian R. "'In Loftiest Spheres': Whitman's Visionary Feminism." *Breaking Bounds: Whitman and American Cultural Studies*, ed. by Betsy Erkkila and Jay Grossman. New York: Oxford University Press, 1996.

Pound, Ezra. "What I Feel about Walt Whitman." *Critical Essays on Walt Whitman*, ed. by James Woodress. Boston: G.K. Hall, 1983.

Price, Kenneth M., ed. *Walt Whitman: The Contemporary Reviews*. Cambridge: Cambridge University Press, 1996.

————. *Whitman and Tradition: The Poet in His Century*. New Haven: Yale University Press, 1990.

Railton, Stephen. "'As If I Were With You'—The Performance of Whitman's Poetry." In *The Cambridge Companion to Walt Whitman*, ed. by Ezra Greenspan. Cambridge: Cambridge University Press, 1995.

Reef, Catherine. *Walt Whitman*. New York: Clarion Books, 1995.

Reynolds, David S. "Whitman and Nineteenth-Century Views of Gender and Sexuality." *Walt Whitman of Mickle Street: A Centennial Collection*, ed. by Geoffrey M. Sill. Knoxville: The University of Tennessee Press, 1994.

Rossetti, William Michael. "[Whitman's English Editor Writes a Friend]." *Critical Essays on Walt Whitman*, ed. by James Woodress. Boston: G.K. Hall, 1983.

Rupp, Richard H., ed. *Critics on Whitman*. Coral Gables, Fla.: University of Miami Press, 1972.

Shively, Charley. *Calamus Lovers: Walt Whitman's Working-Class Camerados*. San Francisco: Gay Sunshine Press, 1987.

Sill, Geoffrey M., ed. *Walt Whitman of Mickle Street: A Centennial Collection*. Knoxville: The University of Tennessee Press, 1994.

Simpson, Louis. "Strategies of Sex in Whitman's Poetry." *Walt Whitman of Mickle Street: A Centennial Collection*, ed. by Geoffrey M. Sill. Knoxville: The University of Tennessee Press, 1994.

Stoutenburg, Adrien and Baker, Laura Nelson. *Listen, America: A Life of Walt Whitman*. New York: Scribner, 1968.

Stovall, Floyd. *The Foreground of Leaves of Grass*. Charlottesville: University Press of Virginia, 1974.

Swerdlow, Joel L. "America's Poet: Walt Whitman." *National Geographic* Dec. 1994: 106-141.

Swinburne, Algernon Charles. "Whitmania." *Critical Essays on Walt Whitman*, ed. by James Woodress. Boston: G.K. Hall, 1983.

Thomas, M. Wynn. *The Lunar Light of Whitman's Poetry*. Cambridge: Harvard University Press, 1987.

Thoreau, Henry David. "[A Letter about Whitman]." *Critical Essays on Walt Whitman*, ed. by James Woodress. Boston: G.K. Hall, 1983.

Trachtenberg, Alan. "Walt Whitman: Precipitant of the Modern." *The Cambridge Companion to Walt Whitman*, ed. by Ezra Greenspan. Cambridge: Cambridge University Press, 1995.

Warren, James Perrin. "Reading Whitman's Postwar Poetry." *The Cambridge Companion to Walt Whitman*, ed. by Ezra Greenspan. Cambridge: Cambridge University Press, 1995.

White, William, ed. *1980: Leaves of Grass at 125: Eight Essays*. Detroit: Wayne State University Press, 1980.

Whitman, Walt. *The Correspondence*, ed. by Edwin Havilland Miller, 6 vols. New York: New York University Press, 1961-1977.

———. "Walt Whitman and His Poems." *Walt Whitman: The Contemporary Reviews*, ed. by Kenneth M. Price. Cambridge: Cambridge University Press, 1996.

———. *Walt Whitman: Poetry and Prose*. New York: The Library of America, 1996.

Wiener, Gary, ed. *Readings on Walt Whitman*. San Diego: Greenhaven Press, 1999.

Wilde, Oscar. "The Gospel According to Walt Whitman." *Walt Whitman: The Contemporary Reviews*, ed. by Kenneth M. Price. Cambridge: Cambridge University Press, 1996.

Williams, William Carlos. "An Essay on *Leaves of Grass*." Leaves of Grass*: One Hundred Years After*, ed. by Milton Hindus. Stanford: Stanford University Press, 1955.

Winwar, Frances. *American Giant: Walt Whitman and His Times*. New York: Harper & Brothers, 1941.

Woodress, James, ed. *Critical Essays on Walt Whitman*. Boston: G.K. Hall, 1983.

Yingling, Tom. "Homosexuality and Utopian Discourse in American Poetry." In *Breaking Bounds: Whitman and American Cultural Studies*, ed. by Betsy Erkkila and Jay Grossman. New York: Oxford University Press, 1996.

Zweig, Paul. *Walt Whitman: The Making of the Poet*. New York: Basic, 1984.

WEBSITES

Walt Whitman – The Academy of American Poets
www.poets.org/poets/poets.cfm?prmID=127&CFID=2310315&CFTOKEN=38513614

The Walt Whitman Archive
www.iath.virginia.edu/whitman/

Walt Whitman Arts Center
www.waltwhitmancenter.org/

Walt Whitman Birthplace Museum
www.waltwhitman.org/

Walt Whitman – Introduction
www.sc.edu/library/spcoll/amlit/whitman.html

Walt Whitman Home Page (Library of Congress)
memory.loc.gov/ammem/wwhtml/wwhome.html

Walt Whitman, Long Island's Great Grey Poet
www.liglobal.com/walt/

Walt Whitman Quarterly Review
www.uiowa.edu/~wwqr/index2.html

Contributors

HAROLD BLOOM is Sterling Professor of the Humanities at Yale University and Henry W. and Albert A. Berg Professor of English at the New York University Graduate School. He is the author of over 20 books, including *Shelley's Mythmaking* (1959), *The Visionary Company* (1961), *Blake's Apocalypse* (1963), *Yeats* (1970), *A Map of Misreading* (1975), *Kabbalah and Criticism* (1975), *Agon: Toward a Theory of Revisionism* (1982), *The American Religion* (1992), *The Western Canon* (1994), and *Omens of Millennium: The Gnosis of Angels, Dreams, and Resurrection* (1996). *The Anxiety of Influence* (1973) sets forth Professor Bloom's provocative theory of the literary relationships between the great writers and their predecessors. His most recent books include *Shakespeare: The Invention of the Human*, a 1998 National Book Award finalist, and *How to Read and Why*, which was published in 2000. In 1999, Professor Bloom received the prestigious American Academy of Arts and Letters Gold Medal for Criticism.

JUDITH CONNORS is a writer and editor who lives in Thornton, Pennsylvania. Her area of study has been in 19th-Century American Literature. She has written numerous newspaper articles.

MATT LONGABUCCO is a PhD candidate in English at New York University. He teaches writing at NYU and Bard College.

RANDALL JARRELL was a poet, literary critic, and teacher. His books of poetry include *Little Friend, Little Friend* (1945) and *The Woman at the Washington Zoo* (1960), which won the National Book Award. *Poetry and the Age* (1953) and *A Sad Heart at the Supermarket* (1962) are books of essays. He was a poetry editor for *The Nation*, and taught for much of his career at the Women's College of the University of North Carolina, Greensboro.

STEPHEN RAILTON is a professor of American Literature at the University of Virginia. He is the author of *Fenimore Cooper: A Study of His Life and Imagination* (1978) and *Authorship and Audience: Literary Performance in the American Renaissance* (1991). He is also the editor of *Walt Whitman: Whitman's Autograph Revisions of R.M. Bucke's* Walt Whitman (1974) and co-editor of *Emerson and His Legacy: Essays in Honor of Quentin Anderson* (1986).

INDEX